The story is written by Maynard's eldest son Paul, who experienced first hand many of the happenings of the book, and studied letters, diaries, and sermons of his father. Paul James is well qualified to write this biography, not only by his home background but also by his training. He holds an honours degree in history from the University of Wales, and an honours degree in theology from Cambridge University. He is a Church of England Vicar and Rural Dean, and is an Adviser on Evangelism in the Diocese of Lichfield.

A Man on Fire

The Story of

MAYNARD JAMES

by

PAUL JAMES

MOORLEY'S Print & Publishing

ISBN 0 86071 421 7

MOORLEY'S Print & Publishing
23 PARK ROAD, ILKESTON, DERBYS., DE7 5DA - ENGLAND

FOREWORD

Maynard G. James was a student at Cliff College during the years 1927 and 1928 when the Rev. Samuel Chadwick was Principal. Over the years he kept contact with the College being a regular attender at the Anniversary (now Celebration) Weekends. Whenever he attended, he led the opening meetings in prayer and so many have been thankful for the way in which his prayers set the tone for these important weekends.

The College is thankful to God that a gifted person like Maynard James is numbered amongst its former students, for gifted he was as preacher, evangelist, teacher and writer. But supremely he was a man of God.

My personal contact with him was during the thirteen years I served in Warrington. He came to speak at the Padgate College Chapel and, at his invitation, I reciprocated by speaking at the Southport International Revival Convention. It was a privilege to have known him and to have enjoyed his fellowship.

It was therefore of special interest to me to read this biography by his son Paul James, particularly the chapter about his student and trekking days at Cliff College. Clearly the student Maynard James and his teacher Samuel Chadwick were men of like heart and mind. The profound influence Mr Chadwick had on Maynard's life is therefore understandable. Not least is Chadwick's guiding hand seen in the evangelistic enterprise of student treks. The account this book contains of the scenes of revival which attended the ministry of those student trekkers and the way in which God provided for all their needs will be a source of inspiration and challenge to all modern day Cliff students.

However, it is my pleasure to commend this book to all who would seek to be more Christ-like in life and ministry. For Maynard James was a veritable spiritual giant whose witness is an example to us all.

William R. Davies
Principal, Cliff College
May 1993.

ACKNOWLEDGEMENTS and THANKS

When my father was alive I never thought I would write his story. However, after his death many memories came flooding back, and I read again Dr. Jack Ford's thesis, *"In the steps of John Wesley"*. A conversation with Miss Pauline Ford, Jack's daughter, encouraged me to further research, especially from the Flame magazine, as well as adding from my own experience. The task is at last complete, though it has not been easy amongst all the pressures of parish ministry.

I owe thanks to many people, and I have put down a few of their names on p. 184, but there are many others. The original manuscript was read by the Rev. Dr. Albert Lown, who also gave me some valuable material, including the draft of his sermon at my father's funeral. He died a short time ago, as did Mrs Elenor Ainscough (formerly "Filer") who also features in this book. Principal Herbert McGonigle read the manuscript, and gave me every encouragement to find a publisher. My brother Stephen and Mr & Mrs Andrew Wright of Shrewsbury also read the manuscript and offered several suggestions. A friend here in the village, Dr. Robert Mason, read the proofs and again gave some valuable advice. My thanks to the publisher John Moorley and his staff for taking on the project. The list could go on and on. Many of the names I have forgotten, including a large number of Calvary Holiness Church pastors and people, who nevertheless are very much part of this story. The book is but an impression, even though I have taken care to check the facts.

I am indebted to Dr. W.R. Davies, the Principal of Cliff College, for his kind Foreword. My father always valued his links with Cliff College.

Paul James, Woore Vicarage, Crewe.   May 1993

MAIN ABBREVIATIONS

I.H.M.	International Holiness Mission (merged with Church of Nazarene in 1952)
C.H.C.	Calvary Holiness Church (founded in 1934, merged with Church of the Nazarene in 1955)
M.G.J.	Rev. Maynard Gordon James
Flame	"The Flame", a bi-monthly holiness magazine (founded in 1935)
S.J.W.	"In the steps of John Wesley", by Jack Ford, published by Church of Nazarene in 1968
Trek	"The Story of Trekking" by Albert Lown
Ibid	As previously

CONTENTS

1. Rev. Maynard Gordon James
1902 - 1988

INTRODUCTION
THE HOLINESS MOVEMENT

When I was a boy I always skipped Introductions, and if you wish to do so, there can be no objection! However, the holiness groups with which Maynard James spent most of his life may be unfamiliar to many readers, and such terms as "International Holiness Mission", "Church of the Nazarene", "Entire Sanctification", and "Second Blessing" may be meaningless. If so, I hope you will read this Introduction, although you may wish to do so at a later stage.

John Wesley taught from Scripture that the Christian's heart could be cleansed from all sin. He emphasised that this was an experience received by faith, and to which the Holy Spirit bears witness. He and other exponents of this doctrine have used many terms to describe this experience, including: "the Second Blessing", "the Experience of Perfect Love", "Entire Sanctification", and "the Filling (or Baptism) of the Holy Spirit". Wesley described the experience as: *"Purity of intention, dedicating all the life to God. It is giving God all the heart: it is the one design ruling our tempers; it is the devoting not a part but the all of our soul, body and substance to God."*

It is important to realize, however, that John Wesley taught a "relative perfection". It is possible to fall from grace, and in any case the person who is "sanctified" is not free from errors and mistakes. Nevertheless, he encouraged those who had received this blessing to testify to it.

His brother Charles proclaimed the same doctrine and many of his hymns are full of it:

For example:

O for a heart to praise my God,
    a heart from sin set free,
A heart that always feels Thy blood
    so freely shed for me.

A heart in every thought renewed,
    and full of love divine;
Perfect, and right, and pure and good,
    a copy, Lord, of thine.

For the Wesleys this was not just a pious hope - it was an experience that could be claimed by faith and for which Christ had died. It was the indwelling of the risen Lord in the heart of the believer so that he could say with St. Paul: "Christ lives in me".

The teaching that holiness is a practical reality is still part of Methodist doctrine. However, the emphasis on a second experience, subsequent to conversion and received by faith, had lost some of its impact by the middle of the nineteenth century; although there were always those who carried the torch for "holiness", using the term in the Wesleyan sense.

In America, even before the Civil War, Charles Finney and Asa Mahan were preaching holiness far and wide. But it was after the Civil War that the holiness movement became established, and one very important landmark was the very first Holiness Camp Meeting in 1867, which led to the formation of the National Association for the Promotion of Holiness. Although its membership was mainly Methodist it attracted like-minded Christians from other Churches. From this time onwards several groups arose to promote Wesleyan type holiness, and by the end of the century some of these had formed sects or denominations of their own. In 1895 a denomination was formed, calling itself the "Church of the Nazarene". It grew rapidly, and by 1906 there were 45 congregations and over three thousand members. These numbers were increased that same year by the Union of the Church of the Nazarene with the Association of Pentecostal Churches (another holiness grouping), to form the "Pentecostal Church of the Nazarene", (although the word "Pentecostal" was subsequently dropped). In 1908 there was a further Union, and the Church rapidly became by far the largest and most influential of the new holiness denominations, and has remained so to this day. Indeed it is now regarded as one of the main-line Churches in U.S.A.

In Britain the pattern was similar. Reader Harris was born at Worcester on 5th July, 1847, where his father was Chief Constable. After a restless period as a young man he became a believer in Christ, as well as becoming a barrister and Queen's Counsellor. In 1889 he and his wife were invited to hear two American holiness preachers at the Speke Hall in Battersea, London. During these meetings they both came into an experience of "entire sanctification"; and a couple of years later Harris became leader of the "Pentecostal League of Prayer", (again the term "Pentecostal" was later dropped). He declared that: "We seek to spread Scriptural holiness by unsectarian methods broadcast through this and other lands." He was always keen to emphasise that it was a society and not a denomination, and he urged members to stay within their own Churches.

Before the close of the century there were more than 150 League of Prayer centres in Britain, and it became a very influential movement. One young man who was greatly influenced by Reader Harris was a businessman called David

Thomas, who had a prosperous drapery business near Clapham Junction. He had a Christian upbringing in South Wales, but he was very struck by the teaching of holiness. He claimed "the blessing" for himself, and he made it his life's work to spread the good news to others.

For fifteen years David Thomas loyally supported the work of the League of Prayer. But after a time he became dissatisfied. Those who entered the experience then went back to their own denominations where the teaching was often denied or played down. Thomas felt that the time had come to establish holiness centres to which believers could congregate on a Sunday as well as on a weekday. He therefore established a Meeting Room on his large business premises; and this was the start of what was to become the International Holiness Mission, although in those early days it was known simply as "The Holiness Mission". Reader Harris was terribly grieved, and he wrote sternly against it. However, the work progressed, and by the time the first Holiness Mission Journal was published in 1908 there were mission centres at Battersea, Penn (Bucks), Southampton, and Carmarthen. David Thomas wrote in the first Journal:

"The object of the Holiness Mission is to proclaim to a lost world the truth of Full Salvation. Regeneration for the sinner and Baptism of the Holy Ghost and Fire as the privilege of every believer, and that it shall be done effectually in every town and village throughout the land."[1]

Relations with the League gradually improved, and in fact many Holiness Mission supporters became members of the League, and its preachers often spoke at League rallies and meetings. However, the difference of emphasis between Thomas and Harris remained, with the League encouraging members to stay in main line Churches. Reader Harris died in 1909 and Thomas paid a glowing tribute to him in the Holiness Mission Journal.

Thomas was ably supported by other Christian businessmen. There was Leonard Wain, another Welshman who came to London to seek his fortune; also Harry Seekings, W.S. Millbank, and B.H. Dunning. These five businessmen became known as "The Five Men of the Holiness Mission", and they were certainly its leaders for many years to come.

---

[1] Holiness Mission Journal, April 1908.

The Mission continued to grow. In 1908 a centre was established in Bargoed in South Wales - a fact which was to have great significance for Maynard James, even though he was only a small boy at the time. By 1911 the new denomination could boast twenty centres although some of them had been independent missions before they joined the movement.

David Thomas also had a close association with the Star Hall in Manchester, an independent holiness centre. There was an annual convention at Star Hall, and it was probably this that gave David Thomas the idea of establishing an Easter convention at Battersea. The very first Holiness Mission Convention was held at Easter 1914, and there were more than 300 present, with vigorous singing, bright testimonies, and forthright speakers, pleading for both seekers for conversion and the "second blessing". Each seeker was encouraged to come out to a penitent form[2], or communion rail, and was then joined by a counsellor.

In those early days the preachers and leaders of the Mission might be described as "lay". They gave readily of their time and money, and some even gave up secular work to be supported by the generosity of the I.H.M. businessmen and others. But by 1917 it became clear that ordination was necessary for those who were to become full-time pastors. It was about this time also that the name was changed to the "International Holiness Mission", in recognition of the fact that the work had spread to South Africa. But the main leadership of the work remained in the hands of the businessmen, and a self-perpetuating executive was formed.

Other "holiness" groups were established in Britain during the first part of the twentieth century; and in this book we shall come across some of them, including the Emmanuel Church which was formed in Birkenhead by J.D. Drysdale, who in his younger days had been greatly influenced by George Sharpe in Scotland.

George Sharpe was born in 1865, the son of a Scottish miner. He was converted at the age of 17, and a few years later was working in New York in an industrial firm with international connections. He joined the local Methodist Episcopal church, and was appointed as a lay pastor to a small country congregation. He was clearly called to the full-time ministry, however, and he was soon fully ordained and appointed as Minister at Chateaugay. Shortly after his arrival he invited Major Milton Williams of the Salvation Army to preach at his Church, and

---

[2] The Penitent form was the area where seekers were asked to kneel. It is also a term used by the Salvation Army.

George Sharpe was so convicted by the preaching that he himself came out to the penitent form, asking God to give him a "clean heart".

From this time on Sharpe became a fervent preacher of holiness. During a visit to Scotland in 1901 he was invited to become the Minister of the large Congregational Church at Ardrossan, and later that year he was inducted as the Minister there. He continued to preach radical holiness, but soon felt opposition to his teaching, so much so that in 1905 he moved to Parkhead Congregational Church, Glasgow. His fiery preaching attracted great attention, but the opposition followed him.

The issue was Sharpe's emphasis on instantaneous sanctification, and feelings ran so high that he was asked to resign. However, many in the congregation firmly supported what Sharpe was teaching, and a hall was quickly obtained for his ministry to continue immediately. The new assembly became known as "Parkhead Pentecostal Church', and Sharpe made it very clear from the beginning, that the "Second Blessing" would be clearly preached. The work grew, and by 1909 a small denomination known as the "Pentecostal Church of Scotland" had been established north of the border. There was even an outpost assembly in England, at the Yorkshire town of Morley.

Sharpe continued to visit the United States, and he formed close links with the Pentecostal Church of the Nazarene. Indeed in 1915 the Pentecostal Church of Scotland became part of the much larger, and now international, "Pentecostal Church of the Nazarene".

We have already observed that the term "Pentecostal" was gradually dropped by the holiness groups. The reason for this was not that they disliked the term itself, but because a new group of Churches was emerging known as the "Pentecostals", with a rather different emphasis.

The Holy Spirit had clearly sanctified the followers of Jesus on the Day of Pentecost, so it had seemed right and proper to adopt the term "Pentecostal" for those who taught Wesleyan holiness. But there were those who wished to take this a step further. What about the gifts that were demonstrated on the Day of Pentecost, and especially the gift of speaking in other languages? One very important incident in the formation of the Pentecostal (as distinguished from Holiness) assemblies took place in 1906 at Los Angeles. A coloured holiness preacher named William Seymour was invited to speak at a Nazarene assembly. He began to preach about "speaking-in-tongues", and a revival of the manifestation of the gifts of the Spirit took place.[3] This seems to have caused severe embarrassment to the Nazarene officials, and that embarrassment continues to this day.

It is a great shame that these twin movements, of "Holiness" and "Pentecostal" could not have worked together, but it is easy to say this with hindsight. We shall see in later chapters that Maynard James certainly believed in bringing the two movements closer together. He recognized the truth declared by Donald Gee, one of the great leaders of modern Pentecostalism, that "the central fact of the Pentecostal experience consists in being filled with the Holy Spirit. ....and this is distinct from His previous work in regeneration as the Giver of Life in Christ."

The embarrassment which some "Holiness" leaders felt at the rise of the "Pentecostal" movement led them to drop the word from their own titles. Thus the "Pentecostal Church of the Nazarene" became the "Church of the Nazarene" and "Pentecostal League of Prayer" became the "League of Prayer".

Another outcome of the holiness movement of the nineteenth century was an emphasis on holiness of life by people who would not describe themselves as "holiness folk" (a term used by I.H.M. members and those of similar belief). Some, like William Booth, the founder of the Salvation Army, stuck to the Wesleyan teaching of the full cleansing from sin; others, however, seemed to teach more of a "counter-action" theory. Sin was still present in the believer's heart, although it was counteracted by the presence of Christ. This tended to be the emphasis of the Keswick Convention, which has drawn thousands of Christians together each year in July, and has had a big influence on many parts of the Christian Church. The Keswick leaders have sometimes had amongst their ranks those who would hold to Wesleyan doctrine, but generally speaking this has not been the case. Similarly holiness teachers (in the Wesleyan sense) have only occasionally been invited as speakers.

In this book the word "Holiness" is used in a rather narrow sense to describe those who follow the Wesleyan emphasis. This is in no way to deny the very real holiness that exists in many parts of the Christian Church, or to think that "Holiness" is the sole prerogative of the Church of the Nazarene or League of Prayer and like bodies, but it is used to save constant repetition.[4]

---

[3] A theology of the Holy Spirit. F.D.Bruner, p.48, 49.

[4] The word "Holiness" is often spelt with a capital letter by its exponents, probably for emphasis. I have sometimes done the same.

Our sole concern is to bring glory to Christ by telling the story of Maynard James; and this will involve explaining his links with the International Holiness Mission, the Calvary Holiness Church (formed at first from the ranks of the I.H.M. in 1934), and the Church of the Nazarene.

2. Maynard's parents at 2 Cross St., Bargoed.

3. *Joseph and Gwen James with their two sons, William and Maynard.*

CHAPTER ONE
A GODLY UPBRINGING

Maynard Gordon James was born in Bargoed, South Wales, on 17th April, 1902, the second son of Joseph and Gwen James. Joseph was a railway signalman, and Maynard's early life was spent in a small, terraced house in Cross St., Bargoed, right in the centre of what was then a well-known mining town in the Rhymney Valley.

The Powell Duffryn Colliery dominated the town in many ways. From Cross Street, as indeed from many other parts of the town, a huge tip could be seen which towered like a black mountain over the area. Like most other mining towns, Bargoed had a strong community spirit. Many of the families were known to each other, many of the men belonged to the Working Men's Institute, which was a centre of cultural as well as social life.

But it was the Chapels which played an even stronger role in the life of the community. Joseph and Gwen were a godly couple, and they worshipped at Hanbury Road Baptist Chapel, just a very short walk from Cross Street. As a young boy Maynard joined the Band of Hope and other activities of the local Chapel. The great Welsh Revival had swept Wales in 1904 and 1905 while Maynard was still a very small child. He had no conscious memory of those stirring events, but they greatly affected his parents, and were to have a profound influence upon Maynard himself.

Evan Roberts was a young man in his early twenties who had a vision of Revival in Wales; and he and others prayed until it came. There is no record of his having visited Bargoed, although he did come to nearby Dowlais and to Aberfan. However, the Revival had an impetus of its own, and meetings lasting well into the night were held all over Wales. The whole community was affected by what has been called *"a tidal wave of religious fervour"*.[1] Many other metaphors have been used to describe the remarkable happenings of those days, including that of "fire", and certainly Maynard was brought up in a home touched by the blaze of revival, and in a sense that fire never went out.

Another wonderful influence in Maynard's life was the love that Joseph and Gwen had for each other. Joseph was the son of William and Margaret James from Ystrad Mynach, near Hengoed

---

[1] p.156, "The Welsh", Wyn Griffith, Penguin Books.

just 3 or 4 miles south of Bargoed. Joseph had known tragedy as a small boy because his mother died when he was only 10 years of age.[2] His little brother Thomas, who was born a few days before his mother's death, died himself a few weeks later; and his father was left with four small children: Daniel, Joseph, Annie, and Ephraim. William James, who was a devout man, had a particular interest in the Sunday school movement, and a talk he gave on this subject in Welsh still exists in his note book. He was a deacon at the Welsh-speaking Baptist Chapel, Hengoed, and he played a very active part in Chapel life.[3] After the death of his first wife he married again (another Margaret Davies!) and there were further children. Thus Joseph was part of a large family, which had received more than its fair share of suffering, but was a family firmly rooted in the essentials of the Christian faith.

Joseph's wife Gwen (née Jones) lived in the Brecon area before her family moved to Bargoed. Unlike Joseph she was not Welsh-speaking, although she spoke with a musical Welsh lilt. Both were fairly small in stature, and a very old photo of Joseph shows him to be moustached, with carefully groomed hair, and a kind and almost distinguished face. His photograph reminds me of the father in the television series of "How Green was my Valley", played by Stanley Baker. Gwen was pretty as a young woman, with searching eyes and a prominent nose, although not in any sense an ugly feature. In spite of their very simple life, and with little or no spare money, they seem to have been a happy family; and this is certainly the impression I have received from conversations with Gwen and Maynard (my grandmother and father).

Maynard's elder brother William (or "Willie") as Maynard always called him) was born in 1897, and was thus five years older than Maynard. They got on very well as youngsters, and their friendship continued all their lives. There was a photo of Maynard in William's wallet when he died in 1969.

But when Maynard was about 9 years of age, tragedy struck. Joseph became ill with tuberculosis, which in those days often led to death. Indeed, Joseph died two years later, on 30th January, 1914, at the age of 45, when Maynard was not yet 12 years of age. The joys of the family were truly dimmed. The First World War broke out shortly after this and William had to go away on

[2] Note book of William James, father of Joseph, written in 1879 and now in possession of his granddaughter, Mrs Beryl Cole.

[3] Ibid.

military service, serving in the Medical Corps. Maynard continued in the local school about five minutes walk from the house.

It was Gwen who felt the blow most of all. Not only was her precious husband taken from her, but there was very little money to run the home and bring up her boys. She was a very able seamstress and was able to raise a little money by sewing. The main income, however, came from taking in lodgers; and into this small terraced house came strangers, mainly commercial travellers, who would usually stay for a short time while they did business in that part of Wales.

This plucky little woman, only five feet tall, was full of grit, and she was determined to win through. Moreover, Gwen's sister, Margaret, had lived next door at number 3 Cross Street; and she, like Joseph, died at a young age.[4] Gwen therefore took the young daughters Nancy and Ethel under her wing, and became almost a mother to them.

It is difficult to exaggerate the influence that Gwen and Joseph had on Maynard. His mother's love, devotion and determination were a constant inspiration to him and he often talked about her. His memories of his father seemed to be very clear; and he was obviously a man he loved and trusted, and also respected. He felt his loss keenly, perhaps even more so as the years went by. In a sermon he was to preach some 12 years later there is a reference to his "Dada",[5] and he often talked to me about his father. Now there was no father to confide in, and this is perhaps why he sought out - perhaps unconsciously - father figures throughout the early part of his life. In these early days his uncles were a great help, and he was particularly fond of his Uncle Ephraim, the younger brother of his father. Ephraim was unmarried at this time, and indeed did not marry until many years later. (His daughter, Mrs Beryl Cole, is still living in Ystrad Mynach).

The loss of his father at such a young age left a sense of insecurity which remained with him all his life. Even with the great faith which God gave him to raise up Churches, to win thousands into the Kingdom, and to be used of God in many great works, including miracles of healing, he often had doubts about himself; and he had many battles of faith. It is important to

---

[4] Her granddaughter, Mrs Margaret Shepherd, informs me she died at the age of 42.

[5] His 1926 Note book.

stress that he did not give way to these uncertainties, though they were to plague him to the end.

However, Maynard was a successful lad, and he went on to Bargoed Intermediate Secondary School where he did very well at his studies, and his class mate, Mrs Ella Ford of Bargoed, (who is now nearly ninety years of age), tells me he was usually top of class. Even at an early age he took an interest in public speaking. One memory of those days remains, recounted to me by his mother Gwen. Maynard made a speech on St. David's Day. We don't know what the speech was about - possibly about St. David or the history of St. David's Day. We do know, however, that the speech made an impression, and the headmaster said: *"Your son will become an orator, one day."*[6]

Maynard left school at the usual age of fourteen, and first found employment in the local colliery working in the laboratory. After a couple of years, he moved to the neighbouring Llanbradach colliery though he was without work for a period. When he was about twenty he left the familiar scene of the small mining town and took up work as a junior research chemist in the laboratory of the Cardiff Mental Hospital.

But what about Maynard's spiritual pilgrimage? We have already emphasised that he was brought up in a Christian home, with a loving family, and in a community affected by the Welsh Revival. Gwen and Joseph were Baptists, but after Joseph's death Gwen began to take an interest in the Bargoed Holiness Mission[7]. It was here that she came into an experience of "scriptural holiness" through the ministry of David Thomas, the leader and founder of the International Holiness Mission. The actual realization came while she was at the wash tub in the back garden! Maynard too began attending the Bargoed Holiness Mission, and at the age of 13 he had a conversion experience at which he wept so much that another boy offered him a handkerchief! My own feeling is that this conversion was the climax of a childhood in which God was honoured and loved. It was almost certainly a personal realization of truths already held. He came into a personal relationship with Jesus Christ.

Even so, his youth was not entirely religious. Like many young people other interests became paramount, and it was not until January 1920 under the ministry of Leonard Wain, a leading figure in the International Holiness Mission, that he

---

[6] Mrs Ford also told me of his "remarkable St. David's Day speech".

[7] See Introduction.

re-committed himself to the Lord.[8] From this time onwards until the day he died, over 68 years later, he never looked back. It was from this time also that he became closely associated with the Holiness Movements, both national and international, and in which he was to play so vital a part.

One slightly puzzling query remains. Maynard came from a staunch Baptist background and held a "Baptist" view of baptism until his dying day. However, he never seems to have referred to his baptism, although he often talked of his conversion and his "sanctification". The records of Hanbury Road Baptist Church where the family worshipped before Joseph's death have no record of Maynard's baptism. What probably happened is that he was baptised as a teenager from the Bargoed Holiness Mission, but as they had no baptistry, they would have used Hanbury Road and kept the records themselves. Sadly those records no longer exist.

4. *Gwen James, Maynard's mother, at Cross Street, Bargoed.*

---

[8] "In the Steps of John Wesley" (S.J.W.) by Jack Ford p. 113.

5. *A Young Leader*
   Maynard in his Bargoed
   and Cardiff days.

6. *Louie growing*
   up with her
   Step-Father &
   Mother, Ben &
   Sarah Williams.

CHAPTER TWO
THE BEGINNINGS OF MINISTRY

Leonard Wain who was instrumental in leading Maynard to a deeper experience of the Lord was one of the "Five Men" of the International Holiness Mission.[1] Thus Maynard not only became on fire for his Lord, but he also became deeply involved in the work of the I.H.M., as it was usually called.

That same year, 1920, he went up to London for the Annual Easter Holiness Convention at Battersea. He had already heard a great deal about the experience of entire sanctification at the Bargoed Mission, but now he wanted it for himself. How it happened is best told in his own words:

"Twice in that Convention I went to an altar of prayer, resolved at all costs to obtain the coveted blessing. Relying too much on emotional surges as evidence of the Spirit's indwelling fullness, I almost missed my Pentecost. Then God sent a Manchester business man to deal with me as, in desperation, I knelt at the altar. Gently but firmly he said to me: 'What you need is faith, not in your own faith, but faith in God.' That timely word was a veritable Joshua to lead me into Canaan that Easter Monday.

"In simple faith I claimed the promised Holy Spirit; and, according to Galatians 3:14 ('that we might receive the promise of the Spirit through faith'), the Comforter came into my longing heart.

"I did not hear a sound of a rushing mighty wind. Neither did a cloven tongue of fire rest on my head. Nor was it given to me to break into another language when the Holy Spirit came in. But my Christian life was revolutionized from that hour. Carnal fear was cast out by perfect love. Frustration was exchanged for a life of victory in the Holy Spirit. Prayer became an intense delight and the Bible was my veritable meat and drink.

"More wonderful than all was the unveiling of Christ to my longing heart. He became the loadstone of my affections. His beauty and grace ravished my happy soul. And something happened that I had never known - the Holy Spirit melted me to tears when praying for needy humanity. Truly the love of God had been shed abroad in my heart by the Holy Spirit."[2]

---

[1] See Introduction.

[2] Quotation from "I Believe in the Holy Ghost" chapter 18.

It is difficult to over-emphasise the importance of this experience. He was a few days less than eighteen years of age. He had experienced the power of God in a personal and powerful way. And he had become deeply attached to the work and leadership of the I.H.M. Moreover he was soon to leave home and become a leader himself.

Indeed it was shortly after this experience that Maynard left the colliery at Llanbradach and took a job at the Cardiff Mental Hospital as a junior research chemist.[3] Dr Ford states this was 1920, which would make Maynard only 18. However, I think it was a little later than this, probably in late 1921 or early 1922. This is borne out by a note in the Flame magazine nearly twenty years later, which states that Maynard left Cardiff in 1927 after five years living there.[4]

Maynard went to live with Mr and Mrs John Price at Cathays Terrace. Mr Price was a leading member of the Holiness Mission in Cardiff, and Maynard soon settled in as one of the family. This was a most valuable period of his life. Jesus himself spent years learning a trade, and it is an excellent training for a Minister of the Gospel to have worked alongside ordinary folk on equal terms. Dr Ford has put it this way: *"From his (Maynard's) background he derived the conservatism of the Welsh Valleys, leavened by the experience of a great, howbeit Welsh city, and a sympathy for and understanding of the working class".*[5]

We do not know a great deal about his work in the laboratory, except that he always looked back on this period with great affection. One experience I can record, however, as he told me about it several times. One day, as he was taking a sample from one of the vats, he somehow slipped over the top, and was hanging on several inches from the deadly liquid. He cried to the Lord for help, and someone came along and rescued him. He had minor burns but no serious injuries. Throughout his life he regarded this as a miraculous escape. Like John Wesley, who was saved from a burning house, Maynard believed that his life had been saved for a purpose, and he became increasingly determined to fulfil that purpose.

If we do not know a great deal about Maynard's work in the laboratory we are fortunate that Mr and Mrs Price's son Kenneth

---

[3] S.J.W. p. 140.

[4] Flame, March - April 1940. p.9.

[5] S.J.W. p.140.

is still alive and has clear memories of those days in the home and in the Mission. There were five children, so Maynard virtually became a sixth. Moreover, Mr Price soon recognized his spiritual qualities, and encouraged him to exercise his gifts of leadership, so much so that in 1923 he was appointed lay leader of the Cardiff Mission. He was 21 years of age!

Another important happening during this period was his falling in love with Louisa Jackson of Bargoed. Louisa - or Louie as she was more usually known - was a Welsh-speaking girl, living with her parents in a large house on Cardiff Road, Bargoed. Her mother, Sarah, came from Carmarthen where Louie had been born on 20th May 1904. Sarah's husband, Richard Jackson, had died, leaving her with a young daughter Louie. Mrs Jackson subsequently married again, and her second husband - Ben Williams - was a Welsh-speaking Pembrokeshire man, who was working as a skilled mason on the coke-ovens of the Bargoed Colliery. It was thus that Louie came to be brought up in Bargoed. Mr and Mrs Williams had no children from their marriage, and Louie was the apple of their eye. They attended the Bargoed Welsh-speaking Calvinistic Methodist Chapel, called Bethania, where they were prominent members. They did not take too kindly to Louie's friendship with Maynard, who even at this time was talking of full-time ministry.

If it had been a call to ministry in one of the established denominations they probably would have accepted it more readily. But the International Holiness Mission was largely a lay movement, and was not very widely known. Moreover, Maynard was such a restless young man, and he never seemed to sit down and talk about ordinary things! If only he would smoke a pipe and join the local Institute! Ben Williams loved his pipe! Besides Welsh was the language of the home, and Maynard did not speak Welsh.

But Maynard was never to change in the ways they wished, and Louie was too much in love with him and the Lord to want to change him either. In later life she occasionally regretted that he was not a bit more like ordinary men, especially when she was left to cut the grass, sort out the finances (which were always meagre), and carry burdens which were usually borne by husbands and fathers. However, she always knew he was her man; and, what is more, God's man. I remember an occasion about 50 years after these events in Bargoed when both my mother and I were quite exasperated by something he had done.

She turned to me and said in full seriousness: *"But he is a man of God."*

It is perhaps easy to smile at this naivety, but Louie became to Maynard a pearl without price - a phrase he often used about her. From the very beginning she was prepared to stand by him through thick and thin. But first she had to wait for him. He was still working 15 miles down the road at Cardiff, and the only possible time to see him was at weekends. But by this time Maynard was very much involved in the work of the Cardiff Holiness Mission. He had a racing bicycle and could get to Bargoed in a little over an hour; but he would often say to John Price: "I've prayed about it and I do not think it is right to leave the work of the Mission this weekend."[6] She had to wait nearly ten years before they were married in 1930, and their engagement lasted about 8 years.

There were plenty of rivals, because she was regarded as a beauty and had a very attractive personality. She too was on fire for the Lord and had begun to attend the Holiness Mission. She became a very able speaker, and years later the Mission folk were to reminisce about those days when Louie spoke so effectively in the Open-Air Services on the main street of the town.

The courtship continued loyally and steadily, in spite of all the difficulties. Louie's parents were themselves a devout couple, and although they never really took Maynard to their hearts, they came to support their daughter's decision, and they also came to realize and even appreciate that Maynard was "no ordinary chap". If Louie was determined to marry him, they would give her their blessing.

As we have seen, he was already leader of the Cardiff Mission and was also keeping close links with the Bargoed Holiness Assembly. He was quickly developing gifts of preaching and leadership which were remarkable, and which were to be wonderfully fulfilled in later life. I have from this period a note book of sermons and talks which were given at the Cardiff Mission and dated 1926. It is written in his beautiful handwriting, which so many people were to appreciate as he wrote to them over the years. Sermons and talks cover such subjects as: "The Great White Judgement Throne", "The Good Samaritan", and "Joshua and the Unseen Captain". Already he realized the value of a striking title. But the content was

---

[6] From recollections of Mr Kenneth Price.

astonishing for someone aged 24 years. One example must suffice. It is on the subject of Prayer, its needs and value.

"Many things are necessary in Christian Service - preaching, singing, exhortation, etc. But praying is indispensable. We must pray or perish. (Peter - Acts 6:2,4; Moses and Amalek - Ex.17:9,11). Consider the answers given in scripture......" He then went on to give examples of answered prayer, with such men of God as Moses and Elijah, stressing that prayer must be made:
1. *In the Spirit;* 2. *In the Right Attitude;* 3. *Earnestly;*
4. *Perseveringly;* 5. *Definitely;* 6. *Unwaveringly;* 7. *In Faith.*

It may have been about this time that Maynard had a clear call from God about his life's work. He had been asking God to show him his particular gift for the Body of Christ (1 Cor. 12:21). One day as he was standing by the distilled water-tank in the laboratory, he heard a gentle voice saying to him: *"For the perfecting of the saints"* (Eph. 4:12). He came to realize that this was God's call to him to preach "holiness", and it was a calling he never forgot. In later years he recorded that for every one person he pointed to Christ for regeneration he led ten or so into the experience of entire sanctification.[7]

Mr Ken Price recalls how his father and Maynard would go out into the open-air to preach the Gospel and give out tracts. They were full of godly enthusiasm and anxious to bring many souls into the kingdom and believers into an experience of sanctification.

Maynard still remembered his father's early death and the fact that his fiancée's father had also died as a young man. He was determined to keep in good health, and he was very particular in what he ate. Mr Ken Price remembers having to go out to the baker's to get brown wholemeal bread, especially for Maynard; and he would often swallow a raw egg before going to bed. This may sound rather fussy, but doctors are now asserting the value of wholemeal bread, and these habits, along with plenty of rest and exercise, probably helped to keep him healthy until he was an old man. In any case, if there was any obsession it was with using the gifts which God had given him to the full, and to the extension of Christ's kingdom.

His gifts were noticed by the hierarchy of the I.H.M., and Mr G.D. Holmes especially took note of this young man. Although Mr Holmes was not one of the original "Big Five" (see Introduction), he had by this time become an influential leader in

---

[7] Flame, November-December 1985, p.28.

the movement, and in 1925 became one of its Vice-Presidents. He was closely in touch with the Methodist Cliff College, which trained men in evangelism and Bible study, as indeed it does to this day. The Principal at this period was Samuel Chadwick, perhaps the most famous of all its Principals down the years. "Cliff" had stood for Scriptural Holiness from the day of its dedication in 1904; and it was rather like a Church Army College of Methodism. Moreover, Principal Chadwick had a vision of young men travelling about the country, bringing the Gospel of full salvation to those outside the churches. He wrote:

"The vision as I see it is to send forth a band of young men full of faith and the Holy Ghost, to preach Christ to multitudes unreached and unsought by the churches. They will receive no salary. They will go as they are led, and they will live by faith. No collections will be taken. No subscriptions solicited, no favours begged. They will tramp from place to place, preaching, testifying, and singing in the street, market place, village green and pleasure beach; depending upon God for everything, and sleeping wherever a shelter can be found."[8]

At this very time God was preparing a young Welshman to be a leader in this very work. The 1930's were to be a vital decade in the history of Britain. Nothing less than the soul of this great nation was at stake.

[8] "The Story of Trekking"
by Albert Lown, p.5.

7. & 8. <u>Ready to serve.</u>Louie Jackson, aged 24 (1928) and Maynard
at about the same time.

CHAPTER THREE

STUDENT AND TREKKING DAYS

George D. Holmes was a man of considerable energy and enterprise. He had raised himself up from being a bargeman to becoming a successful businessman in the town of Goole, near Hull. He entered into an experience of "full salvation" and became a devout member of the Hull Holiness Mission. His gifts became appreciated throughout the International Holiness Mission, and he was appointed to the hierarchy of the I.H.M.[1] He came to know and love Maynard James, the young leader of the Cardiff Assembly, and this led to his helping to sponsor Maynard as a student at Cliff College.[2]

In view of what was going to happen later, it is important to note the deep links that were being forged between Maynard and the leadership of the I.H.M. Leonard Wain had led him to a deep commitment to the Lord; a Manchester businessman (who was quite likely a prominent member of the Mission) had helped him through the experience of entire sanctification; and now G.D. Holmes was treating him like a son. Maynard had also caught the eye of David Thomas himself, the founder of the I.H.M., and he would soon rejoice at the special anointing that God would give to Maynard.[3]

Maynard entered Cliff College in January 1927, when he was 24 years of age. Almost immediately he began to make his mark with both the students and the Principal. He was very bright, an able speaker, with a touch of the Welsh "hwyl"; but most of all he was on fire for the Lord. Because of his zeal for "holiness", and because he came from the I.H.M. he was nicknamed "Holiness James" by his fellow students.[4] He began to lead other students into a deeper Christian commitment; and three students who were particularly affected were William Henson, William Maslen, and Albert Hart. All three were to have close links with Maynard James in the near and far future.

In the October of Maynard's first year at Cliff College, Principal Chadwick appointed him Student Leader, and asked him to stay

---

[1] S.J.W. p.117.

[2] Recollection of Dr. Albert Lown who knew Maynard well in the early trekking days and himself attended Cliff College.

[3] David Thomas did not live long after this, however, as he died in June 1930. Trek p.15.

[4] Flame, November-December, 1985, p.28.

on two extra terms so that his leadership could have full effect. It was during this period that Maynard began to share Mr Chadwick's vision of trekking the Gospel around the country. Indeed, his interest had already been aroused the previous summer when he had joined one of the student treks. As he himself put it:

"It was during my trekking for Cliff College in the summer of 1927 that the great longing came to me to commence this kind of work in the I.H.M. I realized the need of a group of 100% holiness men who would be free to evangelize in the apostolic manner....During the Easter vacation, 1928, a party of Cliff men - ten of us - were sent to the I.H.M. Tabernacle, Manchester, for a fortnight's campaign. Rev. Jessop gave us a free hand, and amazing results followed. Real Revival swept the neighbourhood and scores and scores of seekers were recorded (indoors and outdoors). It was this campaign that really set the seal upon the vision given in the summer of 1927."[5]

Samuel Chadwick gave his full support to this venture, and encouraged Maynard in every possible way. Moreover, the Manchester Tabernacle was the leading assembly in the I.H.M., and its Pastor, the Rev. Harry Jessop, was a well known preacher and teacher and a friend of Chadwick. He was very impressed with what had happened and supported the suggestion of G.D. Holmes that an I.H.M. trek party be formed. It seemed, in the words of Dr Albert Lown, himself one of the early trekkers, *"that the method of trek evangelism was undoubtedly divinely sealed."*[6]

Maynard's period at Cliff College influenced him profoundly and he was especially impressed by Principal Chadwick. He looked upon him as an outstanding saint of God, and this was to give him inspiration throughout his life. When he became a College Principal himself, he clearly had Chadwick as a model. He also established a life-long friendship with D.W. Lambert who was a tutor at the College, and who became a valued adviser in the days ahead. Many years later I remember Maynard going to him for advice on several occasions. Mr Lambert also became a regular contributor to the Flame, the magazine which Maynard and others founded in 1935.

---

[5] Letter to Albert Lown, 2nd May 1934.

[6] Trek p.8.

Maynard was already a fervent student of scripture and a prayer warrior even before he entered the gates of Cliff. The period there reinforced these godly habits, as is clear from his own words:

"Of the many wonderful prayer meetings we had as students of Cliff College, one stands out like a mountain peak. We had commenced to pray in one of the lecture rooms at about 9 p.m.. Later we transferred to a large bedroom on the second corridor. For about three hours we waited quietly upon the Lord. There was no attempt to stir up fleshly emotion; we earnestly desired only what the Lord would give us. Then suddenly, about midnight, the heavens opened and the glory of the Lord fell on all in that room. All those present burst into audible prayer, which seemed to increase in volume and yet was not confusing or fanatical. It went on for hours. One of the quietest members of our group, a shy country student, became almost the noisiest that night! The results of that memorable prayer meeting were soon seen. Practically all the students who went forth from the "upper room" to preach in various churches later that day had seekers at the Cross."[7]

But student days come to an end, and Maynard was well prepared for a life of Christian Ministry. He had come from the I.H.M., and it was to the I.H.M. he returned in 1928 after his time at Cliff. He wrote that year to David Thomas:

"The Lord has laid a burden on my heart regarding the spreading of Scriptural Holiness throughout the land.... I am willing to die that Christ might be magnified."[8]

The I.H.M. leadership had already agreed upon the formation of a trek party, and G.D. Holmes was appointed as a sort of treasurer-manager. Maynard was quite clearly God's choice as the first leader, and Maslen, Hart, and Henson told him they were prepared to join him on this new crusade. There were prayer meetings down by the river at Cliff to plead with God concerning the details of the venture, and they were given *"sound counsel"* by the Principal who even helped them design the trek badge. Immediately after the break up of the summer term the four of them went straight to the I.H.M. Mission at Fenton, Stoke-on-Trent, to commence the first official I.H.M. trek.[9]

---

[7] "When Thou prayest" p.61.

[8] Jack Ford's notes on M.G.J. in Church of Nazarene archives, Didsbury.

[9] M.G.J.'s letter to Albert Lown of 2nd May 1934.

In Fenton they witnessed revival scenes with over 200 seekers,[10] before moving on to Battersea in August. Here also they had a most encouraging response, and they continued to trek for over a year, visiting almost every I.H.M. centre in the country.

The five of them - for by this time they had been joined by Kenneth Bedwell, the son of the Battersea Pastor - put their bare necessities into a trek cart, made from the under-carriage of a small ambulance trolley bought for ten shillings. William Henson was a gifted mechanic, and he had transformed the trolley into a most workmanlike cart which could be pushed around the country, carrying all the basic equipment of the trekkers. The canvas sides of the cart were used for slogans, such as *Back to the Bible* and *Holiness unto the Lord* . The cart soon became known as *"Herbert"* and is remembered with affection to this day by some of the older members of the holiness churches. The trekkers themselves wore blue shirts with a distinctive badge - a picture of a lighted torch, "AFLAME FOR GOD", and a sub-title: "Holiness Mission".

A much fuller account of those days is given in Dr Lown's booklet on the subject. A few examples will have to suffice. Christmas 1928 found the party in South Wales, where Maynard was very much on home ground. Everywhere they went mission halls were crowded, with numerous seekers coming forward. They were very inexperienced, and howlers were quite common, as when one of the trekkers announced the lesson from the *"First Epistle of General John"*! But their sincerity was clearly evident and the Lord blessed them far beyond their experience and ability. Their methods were sometimes very unconventional, and often they would not wait for specific meetings or services but would preach in the open air, or give witness to folks as they stood in a cinema queue. At Southampton they actually led people to Christ while they were waiting to see a film.[11]

They lived very simply, sleeping on the floor of a mission or a hall. They asked God to provide their material needs, and as far as I know they never went hungry or lacked shelter for the night. But it was, of course, a tough life, and demanded both a wholehearted commitment to Christ and also to the other members of the team.

Further I.H.M. treks were organised, though for the moment leadership fell into other hands, as Maynard at the young age of 27 was appointed Minister of the Manchester Tabernacle.

---

[10] Ibid and Trek p.11 - 16.

[11] Trek p.14.

9. *Staff and Students at Cliff College*
(seated from left) 3rd Maynard, 7th Principal Chadwick.

10. *First I.H.M. Trek* from the left William Henson, M.G.J.,
Kenneth Bedwell, William Maslen, Albert Hart.

11. The Wedding of Maynard and Louie
Seated; extreme left, Gwen James. Extreme right, Sarah Williams
Standing; extreme left, William & Emily James. Extreme right, Ben Williams.

CHAPTER FOUR
PASTOR AND EVANGELIST

The Holiness Tabernacle in Brunswick Street, Manchester, was no ordinary Mission building. It had been a Presbyterian Church, and it had a stately spire, stained glass windows, and a pipe organ. It soon became regarded as the main Church centre of the movement, and a leading minister was put in charge.[1]

The Rev. Harry Jessop had been ordained as a Baptist minister, but his strong emphasis on holiness teaching led him to take up work with the Church of the Nazarene (then called the Pentecostal Church of the Nazarene). There were very close links between the Church of the Nazarene and the I.H.M. (see Introduction), and in 1919 Mr Jessop transferred to the I.H.M. as a Superintendent Minister in South Wales.[2] Just a few months later he was asked to become the Minister of the Manchester Tabernacle. Jessop, or Dr Jessop as he later became, moved in larger circles than most of his Holiness brethren, being an accepted preacher at such important venues as Cliff College and the annual Methodist Convention at Southport. With the Rev H. Jessop as its leader, the Manchester Tabernacle became well established, and was held in esteem beyond the boundaries of the I.H.M. For example, Principal Chadwick preached at the Tabernacle from time to time.[3]

It was therefore quite astonishing that 27 year old Maynard James should be inducted there. He had left College only a year, and since then he had been pulling a trek cart around the country! His pastoral experience had been as a lay leader at Cardiff. But the Cardiff Mission was not the Manchester Tabernacle! However, when Jessop accepted a call to the Northwest Gospel Tabernacle in Chicago, it was Maynard James who was appointed to lead this work, with assistance from his friend William Henson and from Pastor J.H. Farmer.

Many people had come to hear Mr Jessop preach, including nurses and students. One nurse who came to the services was Elenor Gregory who was training at the Royal Infirmary. She had been converted in her native Ireland, but knew little of the deeper workings of the Spirit. She continued to attend when the

---

[1] S.J.W. p.112.

[2] S.J.W. p.107.

[3] S.J.W. p.112.

young pastor took over, and was moved by his stirring addresses. Maynard encouraged her to pray aloud at the prayer meetings, and also to testify in the open-air services. Elenor Gregory later became a pastor's wife herself, and served with her husband Clifford Filer (of whom more later) in South America. She still speaks with affection of those days at the Tabernacle, and the young pastor who led her into greater blessing.[4]

Dr Ford has summed up Maynard's work at Manchester: *"He roused the members to renewed evangelistic activity and intense prayer. Numbers increased rapidly in all the services."*[5] Dr Ford also records that Maynard was given the privilege of writing the leading letter in the Holiness Journal, the magazine for the whole of the I.H.M. Quite clearly he was being recognized as an outstanding preacher and leader. What was the secret?

Of course, he had many gifts. He was a good speaker, with a pungent style. He could get people to do things, and in many ways was an inspiring personality. But he realized that all these gifts were useless without the work of the Holy Spirit. He used to get up very early in the morning for a Quiet Time, a habit he was to maintain to the last. He later wrote:

"If I were asked the most important factor in Christian living, I would reply: 'The Morning Watch'. To neglect it would bring spiritual disaster; to practise it will make backsliding unthinkable."[6]

He used to say that he wanted to hear God's News before he heard the world's news or read the newspaper. He realized that this meant going to bed early, and in spite of late meetings he was rarely around after 11 p.m., and he preferred to be in bed even earlier than that. When he was a little older he developed the habit of taking a short nap in the afternoon. It would often be taken in an armchair or in a car, or even on a park bench. Like Winston Churchill, he found it gave him a new start to the latter part of the day.

As well as his early times of prayer, he would spend half-days and even full days in prayer and fasting. This seems to have developed during that first memorable trek, and continued throughout his life. Thursday became the fast day, and nothing

---

[4] Since these lines were written Mrs Elenor Ainscough has passed on to higher things. She married the Rev. Tom Ainscough some time after Clifford Filer's death. Incidentally her Christian name is correctly spelt!

[5] S.J.W.p.115.

[6] "When Thou Prayest" p.12.

would be eaten until about 6 p.m. when something light would be taken before the evening's meeting or activity. Maynard soon came to realize that prayer is not preparation for the battle: PRAYER IS THE BATTLE. He used this striking phrase himself, as it was a lesson he had learned first hand. The big evangelistic service or rally would often bring in the fruits of the battle, but without the prevailing prayer there would have been no victory at all.

There was another secret behind his successful ministry. It was Louie. As we have already seen, she stood by him during the Cardiff days, and she waited for him while he was at Cliff. If she then expected that everything would fall into place, she would have been wrong, for she saw very little of him as he trekked the country for a year. But now he was installed as a pastor it was possible to think of marriage in definite terms. They had been engaged for years, but now life together became a real possibility. Maynard was inducted pastor in the latter part of 1929 and Louie came up to Manchester a few times during this early period. Elenor remembers those visits well. It is strange how small things stand out in memory, and she recalls the very strong Welsh accent that Louie had in those days, an accent that would be modified by many years in England.

The wedding took place on 2nd April 1930 at Bethania Chapel, Bargoed. The local Welsh Minister, the Rev. W. L. Jenkins, was the officiant. Louie was given away by her step-father, who also signed the register as a witness. The best man was Maynard's brother William who had himself married four years previously. There is no record of a Holiness Minister taking part in the service, although I feel sure this occurred. The service was certainly in English, although most of the services at Bethania were in Welsh.

It must have been a happy reunion for Maynard with many of his friends and family. He had seen so little of them during the past couple of years, and now he was with his brother William and his new wife Emily, his beloved mother, his cousins (including Ethel and Nancy who had been brought up with him), his uncles, aunts, and many other relatives and friends. Bargoed was still very much a community.

Maynard would return very shortly to the same sort of life as he was used to, but with the extra support and help of Louie. For her, however, it was a complete change of life. She was now leaving a sheltered home and devoted parents. She was to become a pastor's wife in a large Church in the north of England, living on a meagre salary, and facing unknown problems and tensions. She may have expected that the long absences from Maynard were a thing of the past. She would soon find out that they were to be a continuing saga.

In fact Louie settled down very well and quickly. There was a loving and supportive congregation at the Tabernacle and they took the young pastor and his wife to their hearts. She made many friends for life, including Dr and Mrs Warmsley who were like father and mother to many of the young people in the congregation, including Louie and Maynard.[7]

It was during those Manchester days that I (Paul James) was born, in June of the following year. It was St. Peter's Day, but mother and father were not liturgically minded and I was named Paul. (I am very pleased that in recent years the Anglican Church has made an option of St. Peter and St. Paul's day for 29th June!)

The settled home life was to be short lived. In the previous year Maynard had been urging the executive to go ahead with evangelistic campaigns. Those were the days when George and Stephen Jeffreys were holding their revival services in many parts of the country, with many conversions and healings. Maynard felt the I.H.M. Executive should be encouraging and sponsoring similar ventures and he made his views known in his usual forthright way. The pressure began to tell, and it was just twelve days after my birth that Maynard and Pastor Dan Phillips (a fellow Welshman and also an I.H.M. pastor) led a campaign or mission at Bolton, Lancashire. A large tent was erected at the Daubill Crossing, with the two-fold aim of bringing outsiders into a full experience of Christ and afterwards establishing a Holiness Church in Bolton. The two leaders were joined by one of the I.H.M. trekking teams, and the campaign began in earnest. It is no exaggeration to say it was a sensation. But far more than that - it brought blessing to thousands of people. In the ten weeks campaign one thousand decisions were registered.[8] Shopkeepers reported the settling of long standing debts, even though wages were low and unemployment was rising. Maynard believed in anointing the sick (James 5:14), and there were definite instances of healing. Local and even national newspapers began to take note.

Pastor Dan Phillips was a good preacher, and some of the young trekkers, including Arthur Fawcett and Albert Lown, were to

---

[7] Recollections of Mrs Elenor Ainscough.

[8] S.J.W. p.115.

become outstanding preachers, but at this time it was Maynard who was without question the leading speaker. Albert Lown calls him *"a natural and gifted pulpiteer, as passionate in proclamation as he was in sermon preparation."* He bathed the addresses in prayer; and this habit persisted throughout life. His leadership was unquestioned, and as the former trekker puts it, *"He was the spiritual model and mentor to his colleagues....he was so respected and admired, and such was the comraderie of the teams that submission to one another gave fellowship grace."*[9]

The addresses at the meetings were given striking titles, such as: "Will Christ come in 1931?" or "The Greatest Sinner in Bolton" (John 16:9). Another of Maynard's favourite titles was "The Man Who Cheated the Undertaker", referring to Enoch who never died, but was taken directly to be with the Lord.

As the campaign was drawing to its close it became clear that a large building was required to accommodate the new congregation that needed shepherding. Unlike many modern missions where the congregations consist largely of church folk, this campaign really won the unchurched for Christ. Maynard and the other leaders felt that as these new Christians had come to Christ through their ministry, they had a direct responsibility to care for their continuing spiritual needs. It is also true that they felt they had a truer perception of Scriptural holiness than most of the Churches of Bolton or indeed elsewhere in Britain. This may seem arrogant, but it is perhaps that our present day uncertainties make us think that one view is as good as another. Maynard and his colleagues had received wonderful blessing through the teaching of entire sanctification, and they were not at all keen that the new converts should go to churches where these truths would be denied.

So a new building was needed - and quickly! Providentially, the ash-covered site where the tent was erected was loaned by the local Squire. Albert Lown, who had been a builder and a carpenter before he joined the trek party, negotiated a lease with him, and supervised the erection of a pre-fabricated building holding four hundred people[10]. The task was speedily completed; and on 31st October the first Holiness Tabernacle in Bolton was officially opened at a special service at which the preacher was the Rev. Norman Dunning, Samuel Chadwick's

---

[9] Trek p.22.

[10] Letter of Dr. A. Lown to the author on 16th March 1992.

deputy at Cliff College[11]. The pastoring of the new assembly was left in the hands of one of the most experienced of the trekkers, Arthur Fawcett, who had been trained at the Birkenhead Bible College. He was already an able Bible expositor, with a very fine mind. This mind was to develop even more in the future, and eventually he became a Doctor of Philosophy (in history) at Glasgow University and also a Church of Scotland Minister. But he always maintained his links with Maynard and the Holiness movement, and he never forgot that great campaign in Bolton. Arthur Fawcett was assisted during his first year at Bolton by a young man called Leonard Ravenhill, who was to be linked with Maynard James in many vital ways in the future[12].

After the campaign at Bolton, Maynard returned to the pastorate at Manchester. He had been away for several months, and during that time he had been "living" the campaign. It was no good travelling home twelve or more miles each night if one had to be back at the tent for the 7 a.m. prayer meeting! In any case, Maynard was part of a team and he claimed no special privileges. Very few pastors had cars in those days, and Maynard was never to possess one. When at last he did return home he must have been utterly exhausted; and it would have been quite understandable if he had given up future campaigns - after all he had a young family and a large congregation. But evangelism was in his blood, and he had hardly settled down to the pastoral work at the Tabernacle than he began to have the vision of raising up further Churches. The results from Bolton had been remarkable, and Maynard and some of his colleagues believed that God could do it again.

During the following year, 1932, there were campaigns at Farnworth, and at Leeds where there was already a holiness mission. But the outstanding campaign was at Oldham, the famous cotton town in Lancashire. The story is best told by those who were there. Maynard has himself written of those days:

"Many years have passed since the never-to-be-forgotten tent campaign that was held on the site in West Street, Oldham. Brothers George Thomas, Clifford Filer, Leonard Ravenhill, and Eric Haines were my colleagues during that epic campaign. Right from the start the river of God's blessing flowed irresistibly. Crowds, sanctifications, healings, and amazing prayer meetings

---

[11] S.J.W. p.115.

[12] Letter of Albert Lown to the author, 16th March 1992.

were the order of the day. We counted it a pretty poor night if there were only 25 seekers at the penitent form. I must confess, however, that sometimes I felt a little uneasy. Men and women were flocking to the altar in such numbers that I wondered if the results were rather shallow....it was not until after the tent campaign was over and a virile holiness church had been formed in Oldham that I learned the secret of the amazing success God had given us in the summer of 1932."[13]

Maynard gives one of the reasons for the success - the prayers of "Saintly Brother McMullen". He had previously come into an experience of entire sanctification at the Star Hall in Manchester. Being an Oldham man, he longed for blessing in his home town, and he used to pray: *"O Lord, send holiness to Oldham and may it stay."* After many years of prayer that petition was gloriously answered. In Maynard's own words again:

"The Divine command went forth to a band of sanctified, Spirit-filled men: 'Put in the sickles and reap for an abundant harvest in Oldham.' We were sent to reap what others had faithfully sown. We entered into other men's labours."[14]

Another witness of those days is Mrs A. Bland, writing forty years after that campaign:

"My mother asked me many times to go to the services, but I had no desire to do so. One day, just to satisfy her and to put her off, I decided to go. Actually she was rather dismayed that I had said I would go that night as it was a prayer meeting and she was sure I wouldn't like it. Anyway I was very intrigued by the whole atmosphere, as it was very different from services I had attended at Church. There was the big marquee and the grass underfoot; the singing of choruses and the informality of it all; and I was interested in the testimonies and the message. I decided to go again and again, and became very interested in the teaching. God was dealing with me and it wasn't very long before I responded to the appeal."[15]

As these words were written many years after the event they may be thought to have been coloured by the fancies of memory. But I do not think this is the case, because contemporary accounts tell the same tale of amazing blessing. Moreover, Mrs

---

[13] "Ye shall be Witnesses", the story of Oldham Tabernacle 1932 - 1972, p.12.

[14] Ibid p.13.

[15] Ibid p.4.

Bland's testimony is the proof that those exciting days were not mere religious fervour. As she herself has put it:

"Our conversion has taken us through many stormy ways and good ways over the past 40 years. We were spiritually disciplined and there was a marvellous spirit of co-operation amongst us."[16]

One contemporary impression of those days is given by some verses from a Lancashire mill girl, Miss Farmery, who was touched at that campaign:

It is gone, it is gone, and I gaze with regret,
On the place where it stood, now all muddy and wet,
Not a vestige of rope or of canvas or wood,
Now marks out the spot where the Gospel Tent stood.

And where the Tent stood I can trace every hour,
The spot where the Saviour first showed me his power,
And oftimes I gaze on that now vacant plot,
And cry from the heart, "Oh, sweet hallowed spot!"

It was here that I gave the Saviour my heart,
No wonder I'm sad, with the Old Tent to part;
I laughed when it came, but I cried when it went,
For I found a dear Saviour in the Old Gospel Tent.[17]

Some of those who had been blessed by the campaign helped to form a congregation which took residence in a hall above a large draper's shop in Manchester Street, near to the centre of the busy town. Significantly the building was called "Ebenezer" (A Stone of Help) long before it was taken over by the I.H.M., and the "Holiness Tabernacle", as it came to be called, was certainly a place of help to many people in Oldham in the depressing 1930's, with economic depression, unemployment, low wages, and the fear of war.

It was soon realized that Oldham was a key centre for the I.H.M. in the north of England, and it needed an outstanding leader to establish the work which had been so miraculously born. Who better than Maynard James himself? The work in Manchester was now firmly based, so it was safe to move him from that pastorate. So he and his young family were quickly transferred from Manchester to Oldham. Louie had been in her first home for less than two-and-a-half years. It was to be the first of many.

---

[16] Ibid p.4.

[17] Holiness Mission Journal March-April 1933 p.5 & S.J.W. p.218f.

12. *"THE OLD TENT"*
"It was here that I gave the Saviour my heart". (p.40)

13. *On the march at Oldham*
Maynard is on the right.

14. *The Men's Class at the Oldham Tabernacle.*

15. *A Scene inside the tent.*

CHAPTER FIVE

THE PARTING OF THE WAYS

The first few months at Oldham were heady days. The crowds were large, and there was a constant buzz of excitement. Maynard encouraged the new believers to attend the prayer meetings and then to go out into the open air with the good news. On Sunday afternoons between tea and the evening service groups would go out "fishing", bringing outsiders into the service or simply giving them a brief witness about the love of Christ. On Friday nights they would gather for an Open Air Service in which they would preach and testify to the large crowds who would gather outside the fish market. As one who was there recalls: *"Some listened and were converted, others mocked us and poured scorn on us - some even threw tomatoes....We gave our testimonies, or a short word, others would sing solos or duets."*[1]

The speaker at the Open Air would stand on a soap box - THE BOX as it came to be known. Maynard would encourage all new converts to stand on the box shortly after they had been converted or had entered into the experience of entire sanctification. Maynard was ably assisted in his oversight by Michael Keeley, another young firebrand like himself. Prayer and Witness were the key words during those pioneer days, and almost every night of the week there would be some activity or other in order to build up the converted or seek out the "lost".

There was enough work at Oldham to keep a pastor busy for many years, but Maynard was already restless. He longed to raise up other Churches and he had a vision of revival, particularly in the north of England. Indeed they had already experienced revival, albeit on a local basis. Maynard believed that God wanted revival on a national basis, and again he was pressing the Executive for further action. Maynard was very moved by the way that God was using George and Stephen Jeffreys, the Pentecostalist evangelists, in their large tent campaigns; and he saw no reason why the I.H.M. should not have a permanent Pilgrim Revival Party (and he was very keen on the word "pilgrim").

The President at this time was Leonard Wain, and the effective leadership of the I.H.M. was in the hands of businessmen. In July 1932, Jack Ford had been appointed as the first minister to

---

[1] "Ye shall be Witnesses" p.5.

edit the "Journal" (the magazine of the I.H.M.), but ministers did not have full voting rights on the Executive, in spite of the fact that there were now considerably more ministers in the Movement. (When trekking began there were only six I.H.M. ministers, but by October 1934 there were sixteen.) The old guard were very pleased that the Lord was blessing the work, but they resisted the pressure from some of the ministers, especially Maynard, for a change of constitution. But there was another factor. It was not simply a matter of legal representation: there were also some real divisions of opinion. The lay leaders supported the whole concept of trekking, but there was disquiet about some of the methods that were being used on the campaigns. Maynard believed in anointing the sick during the tent meetings, whereas Holmes and others believed that this should be done only in a pastoral situation, quoting James 5:14. Maynard and his colleagues, on the other hand, asserted it could also be used in an evangelistic situation, citing Mark 6:13.[2]

Moreover, there were disquieting rumours of the "pentecostal" tendencies of Pastor Dan Phillips and even of Maynard James himself. The Holiness groups had used the word "pentecostal" very freely in the early days. For example, there was the "Pentecostal Church of the Nazarene" in Scotland and the "Pentecostal League of Prayer". But as the Pentecostal denominations became known by this term, the Holiness groups gradually dropped the word from their titles. This was partly to avoid confusion, but also because the Holiness leaders did not agree with the methods and teaching of the new Pentecostals (see Introduction). The leaders of the I.H.M. were very suspicious of the "tongues movement", as it was sometimes called. Now there were rumours of speaking-in-tongues at some of the Holiness meetings, and this came to a head when Pastor Dan Phillips openly declared that he had spoken in tongues. It created an impossible situation and he had to resign.[3]

There were really two issues involved. Should speaking-in-tongues be allowed at all? On this the old guard answered "No", whereas Maynard and some of his colleagues felt it should not be forbidden, given the safeguards of 1 Corinthians 12,13, and 14. The second issue was created by some of the Pentecostals

---

[2] S.J.W p.118 and p.136, note 164.

[3] S.J.W. p.118, 119. I personally met Pastor Phillips about 15 years after these events, and he was still very upset about the whole matter. He joined the "Assemblies of God" after leaving the I.H.M.

themselves when they insisted that speaking-in-tongues was the evidence of being filled with the Holy Spirit. Maynard throughout his ministry resisted this view as being unscriptural and divisive. He never spoke in tongues and it hardly ever occurred at the tent meetings. However, the tension remained throughout 1933.

During this uneasy period Maynard continued to do valiant work for the Lord. It gave him a chance to concentrate on the work in the Oldham pastorate, and it also meant that Louie and their small son could have a little more time with Maynard. In February 1933 Stephen was born. It was a difficult birth and Louie took some time to get over it. She was helped, however, by the wonderful fellowship from the Oldham Tabernacle. Some of the young people gave friendship and support which was to continue in a different form for a lifetime.

It must have been about this time that Louie met Edith Thompson. Edith was about twenty years older than Louie. She was unmarried and ran a small shop in Ashton-u-Lyne, just three or four miles from the Tabernacle. She had been an Anglican, but had come under the influence of Star Hall, Manchester; and had become a zealous worker for the Lord. Her outreach even extended to rescue work amongst prostitutes. However, her main gift was a motherly one, and although unmarried she helped to bring up two girls: Eva Steele, who became Mrs Caldwell, and some years later Margaret Caldwell, the step-daughter of Eva. She became a mother figure to Louie and "Auntie" to the James' boys. Indeed she was known by many as Auntie Edith, and was a truly wonderful and godly woman. She could at times be blunt to the point of rudeness, and her increasing deafness was a constant cause of frustration to her. But she was a tower of strength to our family as well as to several others. She had, however, her own times of strain, and she came to Louie for help during those difficult times. It was a true friendship and lasted many years - indeed until 1979, when Auntie Edith died at the age of 91.

In July 1933 Maynard helped to run a campaign in Salford, which culminated in another Holiness Church, this time converting a disused mill in Lissadel Street. Early in the following year the Executive were at last persuaded to form a specifically evangelistic team. Three pastors were released from their Churches: Michael Keeley, Jack Ford, and Maynard himself as leader. This should have been a real step forward, but it seems to have been a time of great contention. Maynard wrote of it in this way to his friend and colleague, Albert Lown:

"A Revival Party was separated by the Council.....The name 'Pilgrims' was taken from us. I asked to be released from the I.H.M. because of the injustice of this change......... However, my ministerial brethren prevailed upon me not to resign for the sake of a name. We are now known as the Revival Campaigners ...... After a very unpleasant scene it was decided to appoint Brother Fawcett as Editor of the Journal.....The Executive refused point-blank to alter the Constitution; so far as they are concerned the matter is closed for ever.......After much inward struggling the Lord has brought me to a place of real calm and trust. I don't understand why things have turned out as they have; but my present business is to stand firmly on Romans 8:28; if I don't then I am indeed a very dissatisfied young man. But, praise God, this is just the time to exercise that faith in Him that 'takes the spoiling of our goods with joyfulness'. He knows - He cares - He will undertake. We commence in Queensbury on April 30th (D.V.). Please ask the saints to pray for us..."[4]

The conflict is obvious in this letter and it was soon to reach breaking point. I find it difficult to understand why Maynard could consider resigning over the term "Pilgrims", and he certainly showed some touchiness. But alongside this human weakness was a burning desire to serve the Lord.

The formation of the "Revival Campaigners" was, in spite of all the tension, a significant move. Jack Ford was to become Maynard's closest friend, and Maynard was never again to have the direct charge of a congregation. It was becoming clear to him and to all thinking and praying people around him that his calling was to that of an evangelist, and the next 50 years were to see that vocation gloriously fulfilled.

The three ministers soon got to work, and a campaign commenced in April 1934 which resulted in a strong Church at Queensbury, near Bradford. This was followed by a campaign at Dewsbury, where the scenes were reminiscent of Oldham and Bolton.[5] The Playhouse cinema was taken over for the final service at the beginning of August. Two thousand people were packed into the picture house, with hundreds unable to get in. Maynard was never one to let an opportunity go by, so a simultaneous service was held in the nearby tent and this was filled with a thousand people. The team then moved on to Keighley, where yet another church was established.

---

[4] Letter of 17th April, 1934.

[5] S.J.W. p.116.

46

But as the blessing increased so did the tension. When the Executive met in October the issue of "pentecostalism" was before them. A letter to the President claimed that there had been "speaking-in-tongues" in some of the meetings connected with the Keighley campaign, and a motion was put calling for the forbidding of this practice. Maynard and Jack Ford opposed this, claiming the scriptural support for speaking-in-tongues (1 Cor. 14:39). Maynard and Jack heard that two other pastors, Leonard Ravenhill and Clifford Filer, had also refused to give assurances that they would forbid the practice. The four of them decided to break with the I.H.M., and to carry on the work of evangelism without the restraints of recent days.

It was a terrible crisis. The newly formed churches were in agony. Should they remain loyal to the Holiness Mission or should they break away? Oldham, Salford, and Queensbury followed the rebels, and a new denomination was founded, called "The Calvary Holiness Church". Inevitably it became known by its initials, C.H.C.

The rebel ministers were themselves upset, but they felt they were doing God's will. A revival movement could not be treated like a commercial enterprise, no matter how sanctified the directors. Moreover, although the four rebel leaders did not themselves speak in tongues, they insisted that they must be free to receive the Holy Spirit's *power* as well as his *love*, while always putting greater emphasis on the latter. As in most splits, there were several reasons for the parting. Not only was there this serious theological issue of the freedom of the Spirit, there was also the practical problem of pastors being supervised by laymen and the constitutional issues involved. Again it can be seen as a clash of youth and age, because Maynard was only 32, and he was older than his colleagues, while Mr Wain, Mr Holmes and several of the other I.H.M. leaders were over 60 years of age.

Nevertheless Maynard loved these senior men of the I.H.M., and Mr Holmes had been like a father to him. They had given him a powerful position in the Movement, and by and large he had had all he asked for. Mr Wain and Mr Holmes and the others were devastated. Almost overnight they had lost some of their best pastors as well as some newly formed congregations, with the threat of others to follow. They would have been less than human if they had not felt betrayed by Maynard.

It was also a bewildering time for many of Maynard's friends and colleagues in the I.H.M. Men like Arthur Fawcett, Albert Lown, and his Cliff College friends, William Maslen and William

Henson, were torn apart. They loved and respected Maynard, but they also felt a strong loyalty to their parent body and to the congregations committed to their charge. With heavy hearts they decided to soldier on, although they were determined to maintain friendship with Maynard. The ripples were felt in South Africa, where the I.H.M. had a well established work, and where Maynard's young friend Kenneth Bedwell was working.

After all these years it is difficult to know if there could have been any other way round this problem. But the I.H.M. was not a broad Church like the Church of England, where different viewpoints and styles could be held side by side. David Thomas had deserted the League of Prayer and formed the I.H.M. The same thing was happening all over again, but this time the I.H.M. was the victim. The reasons were not altogether dissimilar. David Thomas had felt the need to nurture new converts in the ways of Holiness, while Maynard James and the others felt compelled to build up fresh congregations so that revival could come to our land and the teaching of Holiness carried to the working classes and beyond. As Albert Lown has so aptly put it: It was a case of *"new wine in old wineskins"*,[6] and the wine skins were bound to burst. It would be some years before these hurts were fully healed.

16. *The Four Leaders* (l. to r.) *Jack Ford, Maynard James, Leonard Ravenhill and Clifford Filer.*

[6] Trek p.8.

CHAPTER SIX

THE CALVARY HOLINESS CHURCH

The four men who formed the initial leadership of the new denomination were all outstanding men of God. Maynard James is, of course, the subject of this memoir, but what about the other three?

Jack Ford was the youngest, being born in 1908. After a grammar school education at Hymers College in Hull, he began an intended career as a businessman, and put his foot on the first rung of the ladder by becoming a clerk in a corn merchant's office. His plans soon changed after a zealous tract distributor led him to seek God, and in the summer of 1927 he became a committed believer. He was already a member of the Church of England, but after his conversion he began attending the Holiness Mission in Hull. It was not long before he entered into an experience of entire sanctification. When the trekkers visited Hull in May 1928, Jack was invited to join the trek party, and so he was able to take part in that memorable trek which lasted until September. He then spent a year at Cliff College. When his course at Cliff was completed he was appointed to help Leonard Wain at I.H.M. headquarters, and after six months was sent to the Pastorate at Addiecombe, Croydon.[1] We have already heard that he joined Maynard and Michael Keeley to form the first I.H.M. evangelistic team in May 1934, and it was from that time that a deep friendship developed between the two men. For the rest of Jack's life he regarded Maynard as his best friend, and Maynard felt the same way.[2]

In many ways they were a contrast. Maynard was fiery and impetuous, while Jack was more careful and restrained. Although not such an orator as Maynard, he was a very able speaker and gifted teacher. Moreover, he had a wonderful mind. He could easily have become a university don if he had been so determined; as it was he obtained the degree of B.D. from London University when he was over 40, and he later became a Doctor of Philosophy, with a brilliant thesis on the Holiness Movements (to which this memoir owes a considerable debt). As we shall see, his gifts were to be greatly used in the new breakaway denomination and beyond; and his wisdom and commonsense, as well as his

---

[1] S.J.W. p.140, 141.

[2] Testimony to this friendship was given at a Lunch-time talk delivered by Dr Ford at St Julian's Church, Shrewsbury; 4th April 1973.

true godliness, were a tremendous asset both to the new body and to Maynard himself. My brother Stephen and myself regard Jack Ford as one of the most outstanding men we have ever met. He may not have reached great eminence on a national or ecumenical scale, but his qualities were remarkable. He married Muriel in 1940, and in 1942 Pauline was born. (Pauline still lives in Yorkshire and is a university librarian at Bradford.)

Leonard Ravenhill was just as fiery as Maynard and even more impetuous! Like Jack he was a Yorkshire-man, being brought up in Leeds. He had a most attractive personality, and many a lady's heart missed a beat when he was around! He was on fire for the Lord - as indeed he still is, being the only one of the four alive at the time of writing. He rarely kept still when preaching, and as a small boy I remember him striding from side to side along the wide platform as he got more and more involved in his subject. He was full of pithy sayings and memorable sentences, such as: *"This generation of preachers is responsible for this generation of sinners"*, and *"A man wrapped up in himself makes a small parcel when death cuts the strings."*

He had an elementary school education, and when he left school he worked as an apprentice cutter at Montague Burton's tailoring works. He was converted about this time and began attending the Holiness church at Leeds. When Maynard visited the assembly in 1929, Leonard received the "second blessing"; and after an experience of a trek led by Jack Ford, he too went to Cliff College. In 1931 he became an assistant pastor at the new Church at Bolton, and a couple of years later he joined Maynard at Oldham, taking full charge when Maynard left to form the evangelistic revival team.[3]

His ministry at Oldham is remembered to this day, for as well as being a fiery evangelist, he was also a caring pastor. We shall see later how he eventually left Britain and continued his ministry in the United States, where his dynamic preaching and vigorous writing have had a profound influence. In the early days of the C.H.C. he provided real dynamism to the leadership, although it soon became very clear that he was not very interested in the organizational side of the new Movement.[4]

The last of the Four was **Clifford Filer**. He was truly a man's man as well as God's man. He had been a miner in Bedwas,

---

[3] S.J.W. p.141.

[4] S.J.W. p.175, note 8.

South Wales. As a child and young man he had worshipped at the local Methodist Chapel, where his father was a trustee. He had a conversion experience when he was 18 years of age, and a few years later he had been "sanctified", due to the influence of William Maslen who was at Cliff College with Maynard, and was a member of that historic trek. William's home was in Bedwas and when he was at home he worshipped at the local Methodist Chapel. He obviously had a profound influence on Clifford, who joined one of the trek teams, and afterwards spent a year at Cliff College.[5] On leaving he became an assistant pastor at the Manchester Tabernacle, and it was here that he met Elenor Gregory, whom he later married. In 1934 he became the Pastor of the Salford church, and this is where he continued after the split, with Salford opting to join the breakaway movement. In 1937 he left England for work in Colombia, South America, but for those two or more vital years he was a tower of strength to the new Movement.

Maynard was recognized as the leader of the leaders, being older in both age and experience. It was a remarkable team. Only Jack had had a full Grammar School education and none of them had received a University education. But they were all avid students of the Bible, and although only Jack Ford ever became a scholar in the usual sense of the word, they all were men of fine intellect who used their minds as well as their hearts in the service of the Lord.

We left the story at the momentous time when the Four decided to leave the I.H.M. On 8th November, 1934, they formed themselves into an Executive Council to legislate for the Churches of Oldham and Salford, and sort out the situation at Queensbury. By mid-January 1935 a title had been given to the Movement: "The Calvary Holiness Church", and it was during this month that the very first "Flame" magazine was printed, of which we shall have more to say later. Maynard was elected President and Jack Secretary of the new denomination.

It would be wrong, however, to think of this new grouping in mainly constitutional terms. Reading through the early copies of the Flame one is hardly aware that a new denomination has been created, rather the emphasis is on revival and expansion and the teaching of Holiness. This emphasis was underlined by the decision of the Executive to call the evangelistic team "The Pilgrim Revival Party". We have already seen that "pilgrim" was

---

[5] S.J.W. p.142.

a precious word to Maynard, and he was determined it should be included.

Where organisation was necessary it followed very much the old pattern. It was assumed that the main doctrines were as they had been in the I.H.M., and until 1936 the Churches at Oldham and Salford used the old membership forms, complete with Articles of Faith.[6] Even the "tongues" issue seems to have fallen into the background, although the new leaders still laid great emphasis on the freedom of the Spirit.

But there was certainly a difference in style. Evangelism and expansion were the themes of those early days, and 1936 became an outstanding year of expansion. Even in 1935 a Church was set up in Barnsley and other work consolidated; but 1936 was reminiscent of the Oldham and Bolton campaigns. Maynard and his team led revival and healing campaigns in Skipton, Thornaby, Burnley, and Pudsey, with new Churches in each place. Again it must be emphasised that many of the new members were recent converts, probably far more so than in our present day when charismatic assemblies spring up all over our land, but whose members are often drawn from other fellowships. Moreover, those campaigns in the Thirties really touched the working classes. Thousands of mill workers and the like came to the tent meetings and became members of the new Churches.

Tents played an important role in the evangelistic strategy of the new movement. One incident in the purchase of a large tent or marquee had a profound effect on Maynard. A Christian businessman had advised them about the purchase of a second-hand tent suitable for their work. Before the purchase was completed Maynard seems to have received a word from the Lord: "Let not the buyer rejoice nor the seller mourn" (Ezekiel 7:12). But he felt too unsure to challenge the businessman about the sale, as he might think Maynard was a holiness crank! The tent was a disaster, with rain pouring in at the seams. Maynard wrote afterwards: *"I had learned another lesson - although a bitter one - in finding out the will of God in crisis times. It was not to ignore or despise the advice and judgement of older Christian brethren. It was rather to have accepted what, in simplicity, I had asked the Lord to show me from his word."* It was a lesson Maynard would not need to relearn.[7]

---

[6] S.J.W. p.143.

[7] From Maynard James' unpublished papers.

As we have already noted, Maynard's background made him particularly suited to deal with working people. There was a similarity between the mining towns of South Wales and the large industrial areas of the north of England. Maynard believed in the direct approach. He had little patience with all the modern talk of "building bridges". He believed that the bridges were built through prayer, and then you should get up and confront people with the claims of Christ. Moreover, once they had entered into blessing they should immediately become "red-hot" workers for Christ. (It is not insignificant that the motto of the new denomination became the exclamation "ABLAZE FOR CHRIST" and the badge was in the shape of tongues of fire.)

The prayer meeting was just as essential for the newly converted as it was for the seasoned worker. There was no attempt to dilute teaching to suit fringe members. Indeed it must have been very difficult to have been a fringe member in those pioneer days. Maynard or Leonard or Cliff would have put them on the Box! A rather more uncomfortable challenge than the "box" that confronts most modern Christians in their sitting rooms!

The outward thrust continued during the Thirties and even into the early days of the war. It is not the purpose of this book to go into the details of all the various campaigns, except to say that Maynard was vitally concerned and involved with nearly all of them. The tent campaigns were remarkably blessed by God in a similar way to the blessing being received at the campaigns led by George Jeffreys, the founder of Elim. Both men were fiery Welshman, on fire for the Lord. Both were deeply affected by the Welsh Revival, and both used tents as a major means of outreach. Each man taught a "second work of grace" although their terminology differed slightly. Both believed in the healing of the sick, and although the Jeffreys' campaigns witnessed more striking results in this way, there were also some amazing testimonies of healing at the C.H.C. campaigns.

On 10th August 1936 the dumb spoke. This is how Harriet Roberts from Burnley tells the story:

"For 3½ years I had been unable to speak, as a result of a severe illness, and was to all practical purposes dumb. The Pilgrim Evangelists were conducting a Revival and Healing campaign in a tent on the cattle market in Burnley, and that night as the Evangelists anointed me with oil in the name of Jesus, I trusted God to heal me: and he did so. No immediate voice was given, but early the next morning I awoke and felt as if an unseen hand

lifted a weight from my chest, and then my voice returned. From that day to this (22nd May 1936), my voice has been clear and strong." [8]

Maynard James rejoiced at such happenings, because they were evidence of God's power; but he never went overboard about physical healing. He came to realize, especially as he grew older, that God can use suffering as well as recovery. In any case, there was the great miracle of new birth, a clean heart, and victory over sin.

This is perhaps an opportune moment to look at the list of those C.H.C. Churches that were established in the Thirties. We must remember that at the end of 1934 only Oldham and Salford were definitely on the list. By mid 1940, there were seventeen others: Barnsley, Bargoed, Bradford, Burnley, Cardiff, Colne, Eccles, Gillingham, Grimsby, Hebden Bridge, Middleton, Pudsey, Queensbury, Rochdale, Skipton, Sheffield, and Thornaby-on-Tees.[9]

Of these 19 assemblies most were entirely new congregations, and nearly all the others had been founded in Maynard's I.H.M. days and at least partly under his leadership. For this to happen in less than ten years was a wonderful achievement, and a sign of rich blessing. However, it would be wrong to think that the Calvary Holiness Church was Maynard James or that he was the only outstanding leader. Many men and women of God had come forward to play a prominent role in the establishing of these new assemblies. In any case, the whole Movement was based on prayer; and to God be the glory!

*17. President of
the Calvary
Holiness Church.*

---

[8] Flame, September-October 1937, p.13.

[9] Flame, May-June, 1940, p.19.

CHAPTER SEVEN

A PILGRIM CHURCH

*"Here we have no abiding city, but we seek one
to come"* (Heb.13:14).

Those early days of the Calvary Holiness Church were truly pilgrim days.[1] A big burden fell upon the Four leading men of the Movement, and some difficult administration was inevitable; but they did not allow this to hinder them - certainly not in the early days. They were on fire for scriptural holiness, and they had a vision for the conversion of Britain.

The Four were joined by some very able colleagues. I remember the Maréchale[2], the eldest daughter of General Booth of the Salvation Army, remarking (albeit a few years later) on the quality of the C.H.C. ministers. I heard her say: *"What a group of men! How I could do with them in my work!"* From the very earliest days a fine group of pastors joined the C.H.C. By 1940, twelve had come from the I.H.M., six from Pentecostal Churches, one from the Church of England, and two from the Baptist Church. A further three were recruited from the C.H.C. itself.[3] Most of them had received some sort of training, the two main colleges being Cliff College and Emmanuel, Birkenhead.

The life and style of the new body reflected the pioneer spirit of its founders. We have already seen that an Executive was formed in 1935, with Maynard as President and Jack Ford as Secretary. The Executive Council appointed the ministers, and new applicants had to serve a three year probationary period. At the end of this time, if successful, they were ordained and became qualified for the title "Reverend", and could wear a clerical collar. As a matter of interest Jack Ford often wore a clerical collar, while Maynard rarely if ever did. Ministers met in circuit meetings about every five weeks, which helped to give the Movement a closely knit structure. Maynard and the other leaders were very keen that the C.H.C. should not become over organised. They wished to keep it as an agency for spiritual

---

[1] As a point of interest, the first draft of this chapter, including the word "pilgrim", was written before I realized there had been controversy over this word in Maynard's I.H.M. days.

[2] Mrs Catherine Booth-Clibborn.

[3] S.J.W. p.145.

growth and evangelism; and they encouraged local initiatives and interest, provided the truths of the Gospel were safeguarded.[4]

Much was inherited from the I.H.M., and doctrines remained basically the same. The full inspiration of the Bible was affirmed, as well as all the main emphases of the Wesleyan tradition. The Second Coming was made an Article of Faith, and given a pre-millenial interpretation. Baptism was for believers, and was administered by immersion for those who could give testimony to Christ. Similarly the Lord's Supper was to be given to those "who loved the Lord".[5]

Although it was not stipulated as a matter of doctrine, members of the new denomination were expected to abstain from worldly pleasures, and the cinema and theatre were frowned upon. The women did not wear make-up and were encouraged to wear hats at all the services. In the very early days the I.H.M. bonnet was worn by some of the ladies. Tobacco and alcohol were strictly forbidden, and this was even made a condition of membership.[6]

Reading this today may make one think they were very narrow-minded. But in fact they were full of joy and enthusiasm, and regarded these abstentions as mere trifles compared with the privilege of following Jesus. Those who did slip back into worldly habits were generally regarded as "backsliders".

Conventions

No account of this period is complete without at least some mention of the great Seasonal Conventions. Maynard had himself come into blessing through the I.H.M. Convention at Battersea. He never forgot this, and he regarded Campaigns and Conventions as vital parts of Church growth.

In the early days of 1935 an Easter Convention was quickly arranged for the new Movement, and this took place at Oldham. Maynard himself has described his impressions of that first Convention:

"Careful planning, persistent prayer, and sacrificial labour had preceded the feast. In the hearts of the saints was a God-given assurance that the Convention was going to be an outstanding blessing and victory. Nor were they disappointed. Words fail to adequately describe the scenes of glory and power that marked the Convention's gatherings.....fervent singing, fiery testimonies,

---

[4] S.J.W. p.151,152.

[5] S.J.W. p.147.

[6] S.J.W. p.211,215.

flaming messages, earnest seekers, record crowds, and wonderful offerings were the features of the meetings that nobody could help noticing. But best of all, far transcending all else, was the wonderful sense of God's presence that pervaded the atmosphere of all services. 'Twas that which thrilled and satisfied the hearts of the saints.'''[7]

Over a thousand people crowded into the Co-operative Hall for the final Rally on Easter Monday evening. Maynard himself led most of the meetings, as he would in most subsequent Conventions at which he was present. The Easter Convention at Oldham became a fixture for many years, but other Conventions at other centres were also organised, perhaps the most important of these being at Bradford. But the Oldham Convention was *the* gathering for C.H.C. folk. They travelled from far and wide, and the Oldham congregation provided wonderful hospitality: opening up their homes, preparing and serving meals, as well as taking on many of the jobs necessary in holding big meetings. Their blessing was in giving rather than receiving, because as one of them told me recently: "We were very rarely able to sit through the services - we were too busy in the background!"[8] They missed many stirring addresses, but their actions preached many a sermon.

Stirring messages there certainly were, and from some outstanding men of God. Such Christian leaders as Norman Grubb, the Director of the Worldwide Evangelisation Crusade (and son-in-law of the famous C.T. Studd, whose biography he had written); Harold Kuhn, a holiness preacher and teacher from the United States; Reginald Nash, a well-known Christian author; and Roderick Davies, a pioneer missionary in South America. They were joined by holiness preachers from the C.H.C., the Church of the Nazarene, and before very long even from the I.H.M.

Norman Grubb has written of the 1937 Easter Convention:

"The first thing I told them was the conviction borne in upon me during those days that God had a great future for the Calvary Holiness Church. Here at this Convention and in this Movement, I saw the ideal combination which is always proof of the Holy Ghost at work - the presentation of the full standards of the Christian life in an atmosphere of intense joy, liberty, and

---

[7] Flame, June-July 1935 p.8.

[8] Conversation with Miss Phoebe Rudd, who was, and still is, a member of the Oldham Church.

attractiveness. Holiness can be repellent. Here holiness was hilarity! In meeting after meeting ordinary members of the C.H.C. were called up to the platform without notice to testify, and out of the 25 or so I heard there was not one weak one. Each told in the simplest fashion of the profoundest experiences of which human nature is capable, salvation from sin, its guilt and power; first sins forgiven, then full deliverance from enslaving appetite (such as drink in a number of cases), then later the need of heart cleansing to remove the roots of sin still remaining (such as love of the world, temper, impatience, etc.), and the experience of this second work of grace, accompanied by power to witness and live a Christian life.

"As I looked at the vast crowd thronging one of Oldham's largest halls, the majority were in their twenties. I saw the intensity of interest, the tremendous singing of full-salvation hymns to the favourite old tunes, the outbursts of laughter, the evident enjoyment, hearty handshakes, and good fellowship ......Another deep impression has been that the C.H.C. has God-given leaders. The Lord has raised up young men of 100% sincerity, and of large and developing skills both in organization and evangelism. As one who has to lead meetings, I learnt much from them. Whole countries, such as Germany and Italy are in the hands of youth; and it is a sure sign of the Holy Ghost upon a movement when 'the dew of Thy youth' and 'the oil of gladness' is upon such a vast number of its members. A full day's work lies ahead of, and not behind, the C.H.C. Its sun is only rising. The dew is still upon it. Thank God!"[9]

Missionary Work

Mr Grubb's particular interest in the C.H.C. concerned its overseas work. It was too small to have its own missionary organisation, so the World Wide Evangelisation Crusade (W.E.C.), of which Norman Grubb was the Director, was called in to help. Maynard and the other leaders took very seriously our Lord's command *"to go into all the world"*. He had been very much impressed by the scope and effectiveness of the I.H.M. work in South Africa, and he was still in touch with his friend Kenneth Bedwell, who had been with him on the famous trek and was now a missionary in Southern Africa. It may have been possible in theory to have used the I.H.M. for overseas work, but wounds were still open, and it was to W.E.C. that Maynard and the other

---

[9] Flame, May-June 1937, p.15.

leaders turned for help. This was the beginning of a life-long friendship between Maynard and Norman Grubb. Indeed when Maynard died in 1988 I found an unfinished letter to Mr Grubb by his bed-side. I had the privilege of completing this, and received a most gracious reply. But this is to jump more than fifty years ahead!

In 1936 Mr Grubb had spoken at the Bradford Convention, and from that came the idea of linking the Overseas C.H.C. work with that of W.E.C. The new Movement would still retain its own identity, but with the backing and expertise of the bigger organisation. This idea quickly developed, and Clifford Filer, the Pastor of the Salford Church, and one of the Four, his fiancée Elenor Gregory, and George Thomas, who had been on campaign with Maynard and Jack Ford were accepted for work in South America.[10] Clifford Filer and George Thomas sailed in April 1937, and were joined later by their fiancées who were soon to become their wives and work alongside them in Colombia.

Details of that work is beyond the scope of this memoir, except to say that Maynard and the C.H.C. kept in close touch with the developing work in that needy land. Moreover Clifford and George were close personal friends of Maynard, and Elenor Filer had been greatly blessed under his ministry at Manchester. The C.H.C. in those days was small enough to have close personal links, and Maynard would write in his own hand to Clifford, George and the missionaries who followed them. The work continued to remain small in size, however, and never developed to the proportions that were first envisaged, in spite of some heroic work by those early pioneers.

The Flame

Maynard also believed in the written word as an effective vehicle of the Gospel. He had been a contributor to the I.H.M. Journal, but he longed for a *"red-hot"* (his words) magazine which would keep the sanctified alight and set fire to the unconverted. The very name FLAME was an inspired choice for the new periodical, the first issue appeared in April 1935, with Maynard as the main Editor, along with his close friend Jack Ford. It was quarto sized (10 x 8ins) and cost 1d (old penny). It had twelve pages, including the cover, and the first issue had a picture of the Pilgrim Revival Party on the front. About 5,000 copies were printed.

---

[10] Flame Editorial, March-April 1937.

It was a venture of faith and hard work. Maynard already had numerous commitments, and the first Easter Convention was being organized, but he felt it was vitally important to produce a vibrant magazine. In his first editorial he wrote:

"The need for pure, invigorating and spiritual reading is more pressing than ever before. We stand for aggressive evangelism. Our slogan is: 'Evangelize or perish!'" [11]

The first Flame had articles on Healing, Holiness, and the Second Coming, as well as news from the various campaigns and Church centres. The back pages concluded with an appeal:

"Our burning passion is to spread the glorious message of full salvation amongst the masses, and to set up live centres of holiness all over the land. Who will help us in this great adventure for the Lord?.... No pay is guaranteed; no denomination status is offered; but just the glorious privilege of apostolic adventures for Jesus Christ on the very eve of his Second Coming. Count the cost, brother, and obey the heavenly vision."

It was no mere rhetorical question. An address was given for applicants!

The magazine came out every two months and continues to do so to this day, Maynard being the Editor for nearly fifty years.[12] Its pages soon increased to 20, while its circulation crept up gradually and in 1940 stood at 18,000. It followed the same pattern as the first edition, with Holiness and the Second Coming as perhaps the main themes. However, there were powerful articles on Prayer, Missionary Challenge, and other Christian themes.

One very important item in those early issues of the Flame was the Testimony page, entitled *"In the Witness Box"*. The very first Flame (April-May 1935) gave the story of George Johnson who had been healed of "spastic paraplegia" at the Holiness Tabernacle, Oldham. The August-September magazine had the testimony of Harry Toft, who had been an outstanding rugby football player. He was very well known in the north of England. having played for the famous Rugby League club of Hunslet. Before that he had been very well known in South Wales, playing Rugby Union for Swansea, when they were the leading team in the Principality. Harry Toft's son, also called Harry, became one of the C.H.C. pastors and worked very closely with Maynard James. Another very challenging testimony was that of Pastor William Hardy of St. Helens. He had been brought up in a Public

---

[11] Flame, April-May 1935.

[12] Its present Editor, who succeeded Maynard in 1984, is the Rev. Peter Gentry.

House in that town, and soon took to heavy drinking himself. During the First World War he survived the terrible Battle of the Somme, although badly wounded in the arm. He was converted through his little boy urging him to attend the chapel connected with his Sunday School. He later entered into the "Second Blessing" through Emmanuel Church, Birkenhead.[13] Pastor Hardy continued to have close links with Maynard until the end of his life, pastoring an independent Mission Church in St. Helens, while at the same time developing an interest in the work amongst Pygmies in what was then the Belgian Congo. He was a colourful and forthright man of God - rough hewn, but very precious.

From the beginning Maynard would include comments in the Flame on current affairs, and many of the statements were both brave and prophetic. In the September-October 1937 issue, Jack Ford wrote of the plight of Pastor Niemoller in Germany; and there were several references to the persecution of the Jews, and the dangers of Hitlerism.[14] The dangers of Communism and Romanism were also emphasised.

Maynard was determined that it would reach out to the "man in the street" and older members at the Oldham Church can still remember selling the Flame in pubs in much the same way as the Salvation Army would sell their "War Cry" - to save souls! There were many contacts and even conversions through this type of evangelism.

The vexed question of "Speaking in Tongues" was also dealt with in the Flame. In an article in September-October, 1939, Maynard referred to the *"mighty moving of God through Pentecostal people in Norway and Sweden"*. This should be enough *"to convince any sensible Bible student that the true gift of tongues is in operation today."* But even so, "tongues" somehow ceased to be the divisive issue that it had been in 1934. Very few of the C.H.C. members actually spoke in tongues, and in any case the leaders had always stressed the importance of the Fruit of the Spirit, over and above the Gifts (1 Corinthians 13). But the issue was to arise again some years later, and Maynard's position was still very clear.

---

[13] Flame, May-June 1937, p.3,4.

[14] e.g. May-June 1936, p.4,16.

Towards reconciliation

As we have already seen there were still many links between I.H.M. and C.H.C. Ministers, and in October 1939, just after the outbreak of the War, there was a joint meeting of leaders of the two Movements, and a memorable statement was made: *"Rev. M.G. James and Rev. J. Ford and the Executive Council of the International Holiness Mission both feel that many misunderstandings could have been avoided if the Holy Spirit's guidance had been followed more closely in their severance of 1934. Mr James and Mr Ford whilst not admitting that they departed from the will of God in leaving the I.H.M., would like it to be conveyed to the Executive Council of the I.H.M. that if in any manner they grieved the Council in the way in which they left they are very sorry. And at a special meeting at Bolton on 30th October 1939, it was resolved between them that the past be covered with the Blood of Christ, and that a Christian Fellowship be promoted between them."*[15]

The crowning act of reconciliation was when Mr. G.D. Holmes, who had helped to sponsor Maynard at Cliff College and had regarded Maynard almost as a son, was invited to be a speaker at the Easter Convention in 1940. As far as I know, no earthly record exists of the fellowship between Maynard and G.D. at that Convention, but we can be quite sure it is recorded in heaven, where the angels must have danced for joy. It would take some time before the two denominations would come together in full unity, but the way was cleared for true cooperation.

A Pilgrim Church cannot afford to be unforgiving.

---

[15] Flame, January-February 1940.

CHAPTER EIGHT
HOME TIES

During these pioneer days, Maynard became the father of three children. But if this should give the impression of a settled home life, it would be misleading. Maynard and Louie had five homes in twelve years: Manchester (1930-33), Oldham (1933-35), Bradford (1935-37), Burnley (1937-42), and then to Bargoed in 1942. The homes in Manchester and Oldham were, of course, fixed up in the I.H.M. days; while the Bradford and Burnley moves followed the campaigns in those towns. Why Maynard had to move in this way is something of a mystery to me, unless it was that he wanted to be at hand while the churches at Bradford and Burnley were being established. But there were so many other centres, and in any case he was never home for more than a few days.

This is perhaps an opportune moment to relate some memories and give some impressions of those days. I have already paid tribute to my mother and the sacrifice she made not only in being a pastor's wife, but also in marrying someone as single-minded as Maynard. Indeed, he soon became an evangelist rather than a pastor, although he always had a pastor's heart. Even while he was the minister at Oldham he was often away, and after the Oldham pastorate he became increasingly involved in campaign and convention work which kept him away from home.

My memories are very few from the Oldham days, but I have firm memories of the times at Bradford and Burnley, although, of course, memories from childhood can be very distorted. I remember the move to Bowling Hall Road, Bradford, and my very first days at the infants' school. Even the teacher's name has stuck in my mind - Mrs Pride! In spite of father's absences it was a very loving home. Maynard and Louie were openly affectionate to one another and to Stephen and me. This has remained with us, and we have always shown affection to one another: kissing when we meet, even as brothers. This may seem a small thing, but as a pastor myself I have seen the damage done when children are starved of affection. Thank God, this was never the case with the James' family.

Many would say it was a narrow-minded home. We were never allowed to go to the cinema, and Sunday was kept very strictly, with several services, and games forbidden. However, as a young child I took all this for granted, and even enjoyed the meetings, which were very lively. Even father's long absences were taken as a matter of course, and I do not remember my mother complaining in those early days.

Money was very short for my father and all his colleagues. Many in the congregations were working-class people on the very low wages of the Thirties. Some indeed were unemployed; and benefits were much lower than they are today. A minister's wage was under four pounds, and even this was sometimes difficult to raise, as it depended on the giving of the congregations. I remember one occasion at Thursby Road, Burnley, when we were completely out of money. Nothing had arrived from the Church, and father was away on campaign. It seemed there was not a penny in the house. Mother summoned Stephen and myself to prayer, and we got down on our knees and asked the Lord to supply our needs. Then mother commanded: "Look down the sides of the chairs", and so we stretched our small hands into the hidden crevices of the armchairs, and came out with a shilling or two. It was just enough to buy a meal until the money arrived the next day. But we lived well, and I never remember us going hungry.

In about 1938 Stephen and I started praying for a baby sister. Then we heard that the Lord was sending "her" along. One day Sister Lucy Taylor arrived at the house with a word from the Lord. Sister Taylor was a deaconess in the Movement and was allowed to lead services, and had some standing as a leader, although definitely subservient to that of a pastor. She was a quaint figure, with an I.H.M. type bonnet. But she lived very close to the Lord and was on fire with Christian zeal. On her arrival at Thursby Road, she announced that the Lord was going to give us a son. I remember thinking at the time: "She has made a mistake, because it is going to be a girl." I'm not sure to this day whether she had heard on the C.H.C. grapevine that mother was pregnant or that the Lord had told her directly. She was certainly right about the gender, for a few months later, on 6th January 1939, Kenneth was born, and there has never been the slightest doubt about his maleness! We felt our prayer had been answered, although we were a little mystified as to why the Lord had changed our prayer from girl to boy. We were very ignorant of the facts of life. Until the age of ten I thought that God brought the baby straight to the mother in hospital. Pregnancy was an unknown state to me, until I was rudely told the facts of life by another boy. In fairness to my parents, it must be said that this type of ignorance was fairly general, otherwise I would certainly have heard from other boys at an even younger age. This was still a time when parents were very shy about talking to their children about sexual matters, and Louie and Maynard were no exception.

Kenneth's birth was not all joy. Mother was very ill. The two previous births had been difficult, but this one was desperately so. I believe that mother nearly died, and even when she returned home from the nursing home was far from well. I remember Nurse Eva Steele[16], who had been brought up by "Auntie" Edith, coming to look after her. However, in due course, mother regained her strength, and lavished love and care on her three boys. Kenneth became a delightful little boy, and Stephen and I were old enough not to be jealous. Indeed we felt we were partly responsible for his arrival, as we had prayed for the addition to the family - even if God had altered our prayer.

I discover from the records that father was away for at least part of this traumatic time. Both our parents believed that a soldier should be ready for active service and only be diverted by the most serious crisis. Maynard, however, was very concerned about Louie's health and probably would have liked to have been home more at this time, although in later life he used to get very restless when there was a rare lull in his engagements.

Many of the leaders of the C.H.C. came into our home (or should I say "homes"). I have already described the three men who with Maynard made up the C.H.C. Four. I came to know Clifford Filer in much later days, but only have slight memories of him during the Thirties. Jack Ford and Leonard Ravenhill were, however, very familiar faces. Harold Hawkins is someone I remember from the Burnley days, possibly because of a comic incident. He was a pastor of the C.H.C. (probably at Hebden Bridge at the time), and he called one day at our home when father was away. Mother invited him to stay for a simple lunch, which was "Soup in the kitchen". The table was a folding one, and in the middle of lunch the table collapsed and Mr Hawkins' suit received the benefit of the nourishment. For some reason we thought this was hilarious, and for many years to come we had a good laugh about it when we met Harold. He was a dear man: utterly reliable and kind. He did not have the flair of Maynard or Leonard or the academic brain of Jack, but he became a fine pastor - one of the "bread and butter" leaders of the C.H.C., as it were.

---

[16] Later Mrs Eva Caldwell.

It was also while we were at Burnley that I became aware of Harry Briggs. I don't think he was a full pastor at that time, but was a member of the Pilgrim Revival Party. He stood out with his red hair; but even more striking was his brilliant piano playing - I'm sure he could have been a pianist in a leading band had he so desired. He became the foremost musician of the C.H.C. and composed some very good choruses, including one which I still remember;

> *Ablaze for Christ!*
> *A Flame on fire for Him*
> *Ablaze for Christ!*
> *For Jesus souls to win;*
> *A life redeemed,*
> *A life of holiness unto Him,*
> *A life on fire for God and souls -*
> *Ablaze for Christ!*[17]

He also wrote the Children's Page of the Flame for a number of years, and I always looked forward to it.

Another very colourful character was Randolph Murray, who became a close friend of my mother and father. He had a deep voice and was a beautiful singer, who sang many of the solos at the conventions. He had an unusual and rather flowery way of speaking, and I remember him saying once to my father: *"Maynard, Burton's I suggest is the shop for us. I think C.H.C. ministers should be well dressed, but not expensively so."* (This was in the days when Burton's was rather like the present day Dunn's outfitters.) Needless to say, he was always immaculately turned out himself. In spite of his rather butler-way of speaking, he was another outstanding man, and when the unction of God was upon him he could be very powerful in both singing and preaching.

Jack Ford in his thesis says that few of these early leaders had even a grammar school education, but they did not despise learning, and they spent many hours in sermon preparation and in the reading of devotional and scholarly books. They were humble men of God who devoted themselves to the spread of scriptural holiness. Like Maynard, they were prepared to live on very low pay, but they usually tried to be tidy in their appearance and their homes were clean and reasonably comfortable. I remember my father and mother being very annoyed when one of the pastors took a service with dirty shoes! They were indeed a

---

[17] This rousing chorus written in 1939 became, for a time, a signature tune of the C.H.C.

remarkable group of men, and I feel honoured to have known many of them as a little boy, and to have met some of them in our home.

I have happy memories of Burnley where Stephen and I attended both the infants' and junior schools. It was also the first time I became interested in sport, especially cricket. We played with a soft ball in a lane behind the house, and took this pastime very seriously. Cricket was an important business in Lancashire, and Burnley had a good Eleven. I remember going to the cricket ground and seeing the great Learie Constantine play. Stephen and I also learned to swim in Burnley and I remember being taken to the baths by Clifford Coates, a member of the Burnley Holiness Church. Being older than Stephen, I picked up the skill earlier than he did, but I was soon overtaken by him. We both eventually reached competition standard, but Stephen actually swam for the Scottish Combined Universities, and was told he would make the Olympics if he really tried hard.

I find it difficult to assess Maynard's role as father and husband at this early stage. Already, however, it was becoming clear that Louie was the one who paid the bills, looked after the house, and was responsible for the children on a day-to-day basis. Maynard was looked up to as the head of the home and was consulted on all important decisions. However, he came to have complete trust in Louie, and could thus devote more and more of his time and energies to the Movement. In later life he would often say that he could not have done a quarter of his work without Louie; and it is certain that without her loyalty, devotion, and hard work he would not have achieved half of what he did.

The outbreak of war found us still at Burnley, and in the earlier part of the war life went on as normal. One of the first signs that things were different was when the young man next door appeared in uniform. He would later be killed in action; but in 1939 it all seemed to be one big game to Stephen and me. I'm sure that Maynard and Louie, who had memories of the carnage of the First World War, had different feelings.

18. *A scene from an Oldham Easter Convention.*

CHAPTER NINE

WAR YEARS

The early part of the war has often been called the "phoney war". Life went on much as usual and this applied to the C.H.C. as much as to other bodies.

However, the threat of war in 1938 had prompted the leaders to seek to register the Movement as a religious denomination, and this was obtained at the Supreme Court of Judicature in January 1939.[1] This not only gave the C.H.C. some status during difficult times, but also exempted its ministers from probable conscription, although at that stage no-one knew how things would develop.

Maynard was 37 years of age when war broke out, and many of the other pastors were younger. They had to face up to the implications of military service, for though they themselves could receive exemption, this certainly did not apply to the young men in their congregations. Leonard Ravenhill and Jack Ford took pacifist positions, although Jack believed it was right for Christians to take up non-combatant duties. Maynard's attitude, on the other hand, was not so clear. His study of the Bible and history led him to believe that God sometimes used force to further His will, and he was a great admirer of such men as King David and Oliver Cromwell though he did not think it appropriate for a Christian minister to take up arms. When Jack Ford wrote an editorial putting forward the pacifist viewpoint, Maynard insisted on a footnote which stated that believers were free to make up their own minds on the issue, according to their conscience.[2]

In the early days of the war a number of C.H.C. members registered as conscientious objectors, but as the war progressed more and more of its young men obeyed the call of King and country. This meant that an increasing burden was placed upon the women and older men. Very few members were actually killed during the war, although the Cardiff Church where Maynard had served as a young leader was destroyed by bombing.[3]

At the outbreak of the war, Maynard encouraged the other leaders to carry on the evangelistic work to which they were

---

[1] S.J.W. p.152.

[2] Flame, September-October 1939.

[3] S.J.W. p.153.

called; and in 1940 Maynard led tent campaigns in Stalybridge and Hazel Grove, and indoor ones at Sale and Llay. Throughout the war the campaigns continued, and early in the war new Churches were established in several centres, including Bath, Llay, and Sale. In addition several sympathetic Mission Churches joined the Movement, for example, the Old Cross Mission at Ashton-u-Lyne and Holmcroft Hall in Bromley. Three I.H.M. Assemblies also changed their allegiance to the C.H.C. during the war years: Grimsby in 1939, Cardiff the following year, and Bargoed in 1944. By the end of the war there were 31 C.H.C. centres,[4] whereas there had been 19 in the early days of the war. It is an impressive achievement considering the difficulties of those days.

Although it was never quite the same as the Thirties, there were times of tremendous blessing as well as real difficulty. One example of both blessing and difficulty was the campaign at Bromley, as recorded at the time in the pages of the Flame:

"The Bromley campaign commenced on 10th June 1944....the whole weekend was a pageant of triumph in the Holy Ghost...good congregations, a real sense of God's presence, liberty in preaching, and quite a number of seekers.... The campaign party consists of Bros. James, Stillwell, Booth, and Potts (pianist).[5]

"Was there ever a campaign like that in Bromley? Had we known what was to befall we should never have contemplated such a venture. We were convinced, however, that the whole plan was of the Lord, including the time of the campaign..... the first week saw a rising tide of blessing... and it looked as though the little hall would soon be too small... But before the second week started there came the flying bombs - and Bromley lies directly on their course on the way to London. Scarcely a night passed that the speaker's voice was not at times well nigh drowned by the roar of a bomb passing overhead, or the hall shaken by the blast of an explosion. Naturally the congregations fell off sharply, though towards the end they were increasing again..... as an outcome of the campaign we are hoping to be recognized as a branch of the Calvary Holiness Church."[6]

In addition to the campaigns in new centres, Maynard held campaigns to encourage existing assemblies and also led several

---

[4] Flame, November-December 1944 p.27.

[5] The Flame, July-August 1944 p.27.

[6] Flame, August-September 1944 p.26.

other campaigns on behalf of other groups, such as the Faith Mission and the Church of the Nazarene. His diary had few blanks!

Then again there were the Conventions. We have already referred to the first war-time Easter Convention when G.D. Holmes was present. They continued unabated during the War, and their number was even increased.[7]

A remarkable development during these difficult days was the expansion of the Flame. Due to paper restrictions it had to be reduced in size, and the quality of the paper was rather inferior. However, it had 34 pages, and its circulation in September 1941 reached 25,000, just about its all-time peak.[8] In January 1943 its price increased to 2d a copy![9]

It is through the reading of the wartime Flames that we get a picture of Maynard's ministry during this period. It was as vibrant and as enthusiastic as it had been in the previous decade. The articles followed the pattern of earlier years, though there was an increasing emphasis on prophecy. From time to time there were articles about the nation, and Maynard was quite clearly coming to realize that God has a purpose for nations as well as individuals. There were articles pointing to revival as the only way out of the nation's dilemma. For example, Maynard wrote in September 1942:

"England's greatest need is prayer warriors. In the gravest hour of her history Britain can only be delivered by a band of princely intercessors..... who know the secret of binding the forces of evil and of releasing the power of heaven upon a hard pressed Church and Empire... Let us not fail God as he looks for men to stand in the gap."[10]

And early in the following year he wrote:

"Multitudes are even hoping that the end of the war is now in sight... but the Spirit-filled Christian who diligently reads his Bible does not share the popular view of politicians and populace. Of course he rejoices in Providential deliverances granted to Britain in her hour of agony, and he is not unmindful of the high ideals which animate those democracies now waging warfare against the forces of Anti-Christ. But he cannot subscribe to the

---

[7] S.J.W. p.153, 154.

[8] S.J.W. 158.

[9] Flame, January-February 1943, p.26.

[10] Flame Editorial, September-October 1942.

belief (or is it wishful thinking?) that victory is just around the corner and that the "new order" will soon be established. Disquieting factors in Britain's moral and religious life are enough in themselves to prove that God has much more chastisement in store for pagan Israel. Empty, prayerless churches, crowded cinemas, dance halls, public houses and divorce courts are no portent for a New Order."[11]

As well as giving a prophetic message to both Church and nation, Maynard was also beginning to identify Britain with Israel. We shall have more to say about this interesting coupling in a later chapter.

Even in pre-war days the Flame was speaking out against the persecution of the Jews, and this outspokenness continued during the war. For example, in the January - February issue of 1942 there was an article about Pastor Otto Samuel who had suffered in Nazi Concentration Camps.[12] But there were also warnings about the dangers from the Soviet Union, at a time when Russia was very popular in Britain and when that evil monster Stalin was known as "Uncle Joe".

"Europe may soon be rocked from end to end with the blasts of red revolution. Russia, having borne the brunt of Nazi fury, will doubtless claim the lion's share of the spoils on the Continent."[13]

These were astonishingly prophetic words at a time when the Soviet Union was being white-washed in the British press. Maynard was never afraid of being outspoken, and he was equally fearless in his propagation of the doctrines of holiness. There is no doubt that this cost him dear from a prestige point of view. Many who heard him preach during these years maintained that he was one of the best preachers in the land, and yet he was never invited to preach at the Keswick Convention and only rarely at the leading gatherings of evangelical Christians. Perhaps the answer is given in the March-April Editorial of the Flame 1942:

"A letter reached us recently from London which was most encouraging and appreciative. A year's subscription was enclosed..... Our new friend felt the magazine could be improved, however, and went on to suggest among other things that the Flame would appeal to a far larger public, if the particular type

---

[11] Flame, Editorial, January-February 1943.

[12] Flame, January-February 1943 p.12.

[13] Flame, Editorial, January-February 1943.

of Holiness teaching that it propagated was dropped...... But this is, of course, out of the question.... We proclaim the truth of holiness of heart and life as we believe it. To drop it would be, in our opinion, to emasculate the Flame and not improve it."

1942 saw the passing from this life of G.D. Holmes, who had been a benefactor and friend to Maynard and several other pastors in the C.H.C. His death was recorded in affectionate terms in the Flame.[14]

It was during this same year that we moved to Bargoed, the home town of Louie and Maynard. At the beginning of the war we were living in Burnley, Lancashire, but when Louie's mother Sarah became ill with heart and chest complaints, Louie felt we should move in with her parents. Maynard was away a great deal, and there was no particular purpose in staying in Burnley. I was already in boarding school in Swansea, South Wales, and Louie's parents were more than delighted for us to move in with them. So we moved there during spring 1942.

It all worked out very smoothly. Stephen was just nine years of age, and could easily change schools, while Kenneth was still a toddler. The family furniture was put into store, and Bargoed became our base for several years. There is only one puzzling feature to all this - where did Maynard fit in? I have already mentioned that he did not have an easy relationship with Ben and Sarah Williams, although they very much respected him. I have discussed this at some length with my brother Stephen and we both remember father as a rather shadowy figure during this period. He came and went but rarely took the central position that he had taken in the past, or would regain in the future.

I was not aware of any tension at the time, but looking back at it there must have been some. Father never liked taking second place, particularly in his own home or sphere of work. But "The Oaks", Cardiff Road, was the home of Ben and Sarah. However, we survived happily, and "Ta Cu", as we affectionately knew our step-grandfather, was a great pal to us three boys. ("Ta Cu", is Welsh for Grandpa. We pronounced it Taa Kee.)

There was one short period in Bargoed when I do remember father taking a prominent role. It was during the Bargoed Convention. As early as 1941 there had been a campaign in Bargoed and a small Mission Church was established. This really was a nonsense and a denial of Christian unity. Maynard had been brought up in the Bargoed I.H.M. and it still existed.

---

[14] September-October 1942 p.26.

Moreover, there had been a real move towards reconciliation between the two denominations as we have already seen. But good will and commonsense eventually prevailed when the two Missions came together in 1944, albeit under the auspices of the C.H.C.[15]

The very first Bargoed Convention took place at the now united Church in September 1944. I remember the occasion very well, as I was extremely impressed by Miss Dorothy Hoare, a relative of Sir Samuel Hoare, who had spent many years in Japan, and had identified herself very much with the Japanese people. About 350 people gathered in Bethania Chapel (kindly lent) for the missionary rally. Japan was hardly a popular subject in those days when many of our men and women were suffering terribly at the hands of the Japanese. But Miss Hoare made us see them as real people who needed Christ. At the end of the service dozens of young men and women responded.[16]

Another aspect of that Convention was the glorious singing of Myrddin Lewis. He had a remarkable tenor voice, and had sung at several I.H.M. and C.H.C. conventions and campaigns. At first he combined his singing with his work in an insurance company, but by 1944 he had become a full time pastor and evangelist, although outside the Calvary Holiness Church. At the Bargoed Convention he was on top form and seemed to have a special anointing. Maynard used to say that when Myrddin was singing in this way there was no one to touch him! Certainly his beautiful Welsh voice reached the heart.

The Pastor at the Holiness Mission at that time was T.J. Gunter, who was very friendly and encouraging. I remember him asking me to read one of the Psalms (from the A.V.) at one of the meetings. In my youthful arrogance I left out the "Selahs" as being an unnecessary appendage! Much to my dismay his text was "Selah".

But William Williams is the man who really sticks out in my mind. Father had known him for many years, and when the C.H.C. Mission had been set up in Bargoed he became its lay leader. When the two missions came together he retained an important place in the leadership, along with Mr Joe Osborne.

Mr Williams was a window-cleaner and had been a miner. He simply radiated Jesus. It was said of him in the town that if you wanted to know who Jesus Christ was then meet William

---

[15] Flame, May-June 1944 p.27.

[16] Flame, November-December 1944 p.22.

Williams. But it is strange how the little and unimportant things remain in one's mind. His first wife died and he married another member of the congregation - a Mrs Jones. Shortly after the wedding he was giving out the notices, and boldly announced that the Women's meeting that week would be taken by Mrs Jones! We hope she forgave him, but we boys thought it was a great joke. William's brother, Ben, was an eccentric man who would shout "Hallelujah" at the most inappropriate times of the service. He fell asleep once during a sermon by Pastor Tom Food (the successor to Gunter), and woke up when Mr Food was saying some very solemn words about the fate of Hitler. I don't think Ben had heard a word of what was said, but he shouted "Hallelujah" just the same! But to return to William Williams. Maynard thought very highly of him, and Louie also regarded Mr and Mrs Williams as very dear friends. Pastors came and went but men like Mr Williams and Mr Osborne kept the Mission together for many years.

We were in Bargoed when the war came to an end, and I vividly remember the celebrations of VE day and VJ day, with singing and dancing in the streets. Stephen and I had a great time and rejoiced with the many thousands of the town. There were bands, choirs, and public displays, as well as the visit of the local hero, Cpl. Chapman, V.C.

An important development during the war was the move towards unity amongst the Holiness groups. Mr J.D. Drysdale from Emmanuel, Birkenhead, called together leaders from the Holiness movements in Britain; and they met for a Prayer Conference at Birkenhead in April 1942. As a result a National Holiness Association was formed which included the Calvary Holiness Church, the International Holiness Mission, and the Church of the Nazarene.[17]

This was not only a move which would lead to fuller unity after the war, it was also a sign of the developing friendship between Maynard and J.D. Drysdale. Strangely enough J.D. himself never fully identified himself with the movement towards unity, even though he had initiated the Conference. I think he was too much of an individualist. As a young man he had refused to become a member of the League of Prayer, even though the centre at Ardrossan of which he had charge had been linked to that movement.[18] However, this independence of mind did not

---

[17] S.J.W. p.159.

[18] J.D. Drysdale by Norman Grubb p.49.

interfere with his friendship with Maynard and Jack Ford. He had established his missionary training Bible college at Birkenhead, and this college was to prove a rich supply source for the C.H.C. and other Holiness bodies.

In the summer of 1943, when the war was at its height, J.D. Drysdale and Maynard took part in the very first Irish Evangelistic Band Convention in Bundoran in neutral Eire. The Flame speaks of it in glowing terms:

"Rarely has the President (M.G.J.) been to such unique gatherings. Day after day the tide of Spirit rose until the high water mark was reached on the sixth evening of the convention. The glorious truths of Sanctification, the Second Coming of Christ, and the challenge of World Evangelization were faithfully and powerfully preached."[19]

This was also the period when Maynard forged many links of friendship with Irish Christians. Frank Marshall was the leader of the Irish Evangelistic Band, an interdenominational holiness body, mainly from the North of Ireland, but also ready to establish work in the Republic.

Other friendships were made during these years of the war, including links with two outstanding men of the period: W.E. Sangster and Martyn Lloyd-Jones. Maynard differed from them in many ways, but there was somehow a meeting of spirits, and correspondence developed with both men. Dr Lloyd Jones was to comment very favourably on some of Maynard's writings, and Dr. Sangster and Maynard maintained correspondence right up to Dr. Sangster's death in 1960. Their friendship survived the Holiness outcry against Dr. Sangster's book, "The Path to Perfection", in which Sangster seemed to suggest that verbal witness should not be made to the experience of sanctification, as the life should speak for itself. Maynard wrote a fiercely critical editorial about the book in the Flame.[20], but Sangster was too big a man to let this break a friendship. Their correspondence continued, and he wrote to Maynard shortly before his death in 1960:

"My dear Brother, I am so grateful for your kind concern and prayers. The doctors have no answer to my need. But my hope is in God and he was never dearer to me than now...I turn all my

---

[19] Flame, September-October 1943 p.22.

[20] Flame, May-June 1943.

thoughts of you into prayer. Most warmly yours. W.E. Sangster"[21]

Yet another friendship of those days was with Rees Howells of Swansea. Maynard had met him before the war, and an immediate bond was formed between the two men. He suggested to Maynard that he send his children to the school which he had founded, and consequently I went there in the September of 1941. Rees Howells has been written about by Norman Grubb,[22] and most of our readers will know of his great exploits of faith and his remarkable gift of intercession. Maynard admired him tremendously although he did not always agree with some of his ideas. When Rees Howells died in 1950 Maynard continued friendship with his son Samuel. Mr Samuel, as we knew him at school, is one of God's most gracious saints and Maynard loved him dearly.

It must not be thought, however, that Maynard cultivated links only with outstanding leaders. Many Christians up and down the land received letters of encouragement from Maynard, even though their names may be unknown. With all his business he found time to make and keep friendships.

An important development during the closing days of the war was the formation of the publishing unit of the Calvary Holiness Church. Pastor Cyril Pass, who was in charge of the Ashton Mission, and Harold Hawkins were the prime movers, and they both wrote booklets which were published by the Pilgrim Publishing House. Maynard's very first book was written during this period and was published by the PPH in 1945.

The book, significantly, was called "Evangelize" as this was a burning theme of Maynard's ministry. It was the outcome of a paper that Maynard had given at a Conference at Emmanuel, Birkenhead, in April 1944. The book began with the raison d'etre of Evangelism, and went on to deal with both the difficulties and opportunities. Fragments of Church history were presented, including illustrations from such a wide variety of church leaders as Francis of Assisi and George Jeffreys! There was great emphasis on open air work and prayer - a reminder of those early days at Oldham.

The book did not have a large circulation, but it made an impact at the time, and was to whet Maynard's appetite for further writing.

---

[21] dated 27th April 1960.

[22] "Rees Howells, Intercessor" N. Grubb, Lutterworth Press.

The writing of this book was one of Maynard's last jobs during the war. They had not been unfruitful years; and, considering the tremendous difficulties, much had been achieved. Perhaps it is best to let Maynard speak for himself:

"At present we are a young Society, barely eleven years old. We are essentially a fellowship of believers who stand for the truth of full salvation. We exist only to spread throughout the world the message of complete deliverance from all sin..... To reach the Christless masses was the compelling urge of our revival parties in the early days of our history....... That is why we urge our Assemblies to go forth boldly into the open-air, witnessing to the unchurched multitudes, of an uttermost salvation in Jesus Christ. We have surely come to the Kingdom for such a time as this. Let us not fail in our God appointed tasks." [23]

Maynard and the C.H.C. certainly ended the war in a positive mood.

19. <u>A party at the Bargoed Mission.</u>
Mrs Gwen James, Maynard's mother is seated far right.
William Williams is standing fifth from left.

---

[23] Flame, May-June 1945 p.31.

CHAPTER TEN
"CONSOLIDATION AND FRUSTRATION"
POST WAR YEARS

Someone from Oldham has written: *"It was never the same after the War. Somehow people were more hard and cynical."* But Maynard continued his intense work of Church visitation, conventions, and campaigns. There were very few gaps in his diary. He realized that days were difficult and in November 1945 he called together all the pastors of the Movement for four days of prayer. It was a time of real blessing, as he himself wrote:

"In those never-to-be-forgotten seasons of intercession the Calvary Holiness Church seemed to be born anew and recommissioned to the supreme task of spreading scriptural holiness to the ends of the earth in the shortest possible time. The ministers were fused together in holy love and filled with a greater determination than ever to help each other in pushing the battle to the gate."[1]

Dr. Ford has aptly described these years as "consolidation and frustration". Some very solid work was achieved while at the same time there were many set-backs.

The Flame had another very thriving period; and the appointment of Miss Eleanor Howarth as Flame Secretary in September 1945 proved to be a great blessing both to Maynard and many others. It was a job she was to hold with great devotion for 30 years, until failing health and eyesight compelled her to hand over the job to a new Secretary. Maynard greatly valued her help, and as he later wrote: *"Without Sister Howarth's loving and loyal service it would have been almost impossible for The Flame to have maintained its world-wide ministry for four decades."*[2] The circulation was large when she started her work, but it grew to 20,000 in 1949, and to 22,000 the following year.

The Flame continued to have the usual trenchant articles and editorials; and during this period Maynard was frequently calling for repentance. He saw many signs of decline in society, and warned of the dire consequences if the nation did not return to the Lord. We have lived to see many of those warnings fulfilled.

We have already noted that Cyril Pass, the pastor of the Ashton Church, was a born organizer and had helped to form the Pilgrim

---

[1] Flame, Editorial January-February 1946.

[2] Flame, August-September 1975, p.30.

Publishing House. He was also instrumental in helping to tidy up much of the organizational side of the C.H.C., and as Dr Ford has written: *"He multiplied offices and seats on committees and played a major part in the developing organization of the youthful society."*[3] Maynard was not very interested in organization for its own sake. He was a born pioneer and evangelist, and was quite happy to leave the details of organization to others. We shall see that this led to some real difficulties, but it also had advantages. Maynard's single-mindedness enabled him to get on with the work which suited him.

In 1947 he published his second book, entitled: "Facing the Issue". It was priced two shillings and sixpence, and soon sold a thousand copies. The first chapter was on the subject of "speaking in tongues" and again emphasized that this gift is not the infallible sign of being filled with the Spirit, but nevertheless should not be ignored or suppressed. Other subjects included, Sanctification, Judgement, The Second Coming, Hell, and Life after Death. It was written in a chatty style, with lots of sermon-type illustrations. Indeed I remember Louie teasing him that he had printed his best sermons and would not be able to preach them again!

Perhaps the most important development at this time was the founding of the Beech Lawn Bible College. When the war finished Maynard and Louie were still living at Bargoed, but with the death of Louie's mother they felt free to move, and the next home was to be the new college at Uppermill in the West Riding of Yorkshire, only a few miles from Oldham which was still the C.H.C.'s most important centre.

Maynard had longed for "a college of our own". The Movement had benefitted greatly from the services of Cliff College and Emmanuel. But the former was a Methodist College and the second specialized in preparing men and women for work overseas. Moreover, in spite of the high standard of most of the C.H.C. ministers there had been a few who were not suitable. Maynard felt that this problem would be avoided if there could be some oversight in the training of the pastors.[4] He, Jack Ford and the other leaders believed that they should train ministers and leaders for work in the C.H.C., and it was with this aim that the House was purchased in Uppermill. The opening ceremony was on February 11th, 1947, with seven students and Maynard

---

[3] S.J.W. p.161.

[4] Notes of Louie James, written about 1949.

as resident Principal. All the other lecturers were non-resident. The building soon proved to be too small, and the following year a much larger building was purchased in Stalybridge, just a few miles away in Cheshire, but even closer to Oldham and within easy reach of Manchester. The new "Beech Lawn", the name by which the College was known in both Uppermill and Stalybridge, was to fulfil a most useful role in the life of the young denomination.

The course consisted of Bible Studies, Church History, Pastoralia, Evangelism, and kindred subjects. A fine team of lecturers visited the College, including C.H.C. pastors Cyril Pass, Jack Ford, George Deakin, Clifford Filer, and Harold Hawkins. There were also lecturers from other denominations including the Rev. Percy Hassam, a Methodist Minister, and Pastor James Taylor, an outstanding Methodist Local Preacher, and the Rev. Samuel May, the Vicar of nearby Godley, Hyde. An occasional lecturer was the distinguished Professor F.F. Bruce, perhaps the leading conservative biblical scholar of that period, certainly in Britain. Down the years there was, of course, a gradual change of lecturers, and they usually gave their services free, bringing careful scholarship to eager young men.

The theology was very conservative; and the word "fundamentalist"[5] was unashamedly used. Nevertheless, some account of modern scholarship was made. I was at university at the time, and I was rather troubled by some lectures I was attending in which it was suggested that Mark's Gospel was written first and then copied by Luke and Matthew, who also added their own sources. I remember sharing the problem with Cyril Pass. To my astonishment he pointed out that this theory in no way conflicted with the inspiration of scripture, and he showed me some of his own lecture notes which explained the matter. It was a great release for me.

A humorous verse written at the time sums up the life in the College in those early days:

> The Beech Lawn Bible College stands
> A beacon in a pilgrim land.
> The Principal is known by name
> To all the readers of the Flame.
> The students all with one accord
> Enjoy Church Hist'ry by Rev. Ford,

---

[5] The word did not have the suggestion of fanaticism that it carries today. It simply meant "a belief in the fundamentals of the faith".

Homiletics and a meeting
By Pastors Hassam and G. Deakin.
"The Godley Vicar", once a week
Takes us in New Testament Greek.
Mr Hawkins' Bible Background,
And Mr Taylor's studies-sound,
Are enjoyed by all around.

But the subject that's a piler
Is Theology by Filer!
Then see our Matron and the Cook
Who feed us well - judge by our look.
A band of happy students we,
Who love the Lord, and mean to be
Of purpose firm - to set men free.[6]

As the verse acknowledges, the College owed much to a loyal and devoted domestic staff, who lived on the premises, and received only a small salary. They made it possible to run the College on a shoe-string, and they also brought much love and care to sometimes lonely young men.

Prayer played a big part in the life of the College. Maynard believed that nothing could be achieved without prayer, and consequently it was made a priority. There was also a concern for the community around the College, and most Friday evenings the College would be thrown open for a drawing-room meeting. This was often packed out as the students and staff took part in a vibrant service, with testimonies, songs, and warm fellowship. Louie was a key figure in these Friday meetings, busy preparing cups of tea, giving a warm welcome to the visitors, and occasionally giving a testimony or leading in prayer. She was often called on to help in counselling those who had responded to the appeal.

Maynard was by no means a natural Principal. He was every inch an evangelist, and he only took the job on because of the need to train ministers. Nevertheless, his enthusiasm and pioneering spirit were invaluable in the early days of the College. Maynard's first period as Principal was from 1947 to 1950, and by the end of this period there were 16 students. Although the numbers remained small, several of those early students are now full time pastors and church leaders who have given many years service to the work of the Lord. If I mention a few names, it is only because they are the ones that come to mind - others should

---

[6] Norman Ellison, Flame, March-April 1949, p.25.

be equally remembered. Robert Cheesmur is the one who stands out most in my memory, as he was quite outstanding even in those days. He was cheerful, very friendly, and with a good mind. He has served for many years in Canada. But I could also speak of Bro's Spence, McNeil, and Weatherill, all of whom have served the Lord in the Holiness Movement. (They were nearly always known as Bro's.) Norman Ellison is another I clearly remember - he had a radiance about him, even as a student.

The Post-War Conventions were outstanding, although the Campaigns rarely achieved their pre-war successes. The Conventions still had their enthusiastic large crowds. Oldham remained the venue for the Easter Convention, which was the most important of the Holiness conventions. I will recount just three of them.

The first was shortly after the war, during the Easter of 1946. The main speaker was the Maréchale[7], the eldest daughter of the great William Booth of the Salvation Army. She was by this time an old lady in her eighties, but still full of Holy Ghost fire. Her sermons were full of pithy sayings, such as: "*You cannot know Christ without his Cross.*", and "*You can tell a person's love for the Lord by the distance between him and the lost.*" As a young woman she had worked with the Salvation Army in Paris where she had broken down prejudice and fear in some of the toughest parts of the city. The people of Paris nick-named her "Maréchale" when her earlier title of "Capitaine" was superseded by higher rank! I shall never forget this grand old lady, and I still have the book she gave to Maynard, which was inscribed: "*In memory of valuable help during a blessed campaign in Oldham, April 1946. How can we save a dying world? That problem has been solved above; the Key is found at Calvary, the only way is Love. Maréchale.*"

I have already mentioned her complimentary remarks about C.H.C. pastors, which I heard her say at one of the meetings; and she added something like: "*What I could do with such a group of men for God's work!*"

The second Convention which comes to mind was in 1948. The main speaker was evangelist W.P. Nicholson. He was at this time a household name amongst Protestants in Northern Ireland, but was not so well-known in England, in spite of his taking part in a famous Mission at Cambridge University in 1926, when his blunt ways had caused a sensation. On one occasion he had

---

[7] Mrs Catherine Booth-Cibborn.

complained that there were too many hypocrites in the service; and a College Chaplain wrote to the President of the Christian Union complaining that he had been called a hypocrite! But his blunt preaching had results and there were a number of converts, including the Secretary of the University Drunks' club, who later became Secretary of a missionary society!

At the Oldham Convention it was the same and some were offended by him. I remember him being very rude to a man who had to leave a meeting in an emergency. But equally he roused others with his direct challenge.

The following year, 1949, was a complete contrast. An American lady named Miss Nettie Miller, from the Church of the Nazarene in America, came like a bombshell. As I have said in a previous chapter, the Holiness folk of those days tended to be rather severe in their dress; and in any case the post-war years were very austere and clothes were rationed. Nettie, however, might have stepped out of a Hollywood film. This was still the days of the big stars of the cinema screen, and Nettie was something of a star. She told me she had been offered a contract by a Hollywood company, and although I have never been able to check this, I have no reason to doubt it. She took an immediate liking to Stephen and me, and treated us like young brothers. I shall never forget walking down the main street of Ashton-u-Lyne, which in those days was very drab, with this highly glamorous woman on my arm. People actually stopped and stared! It might have been Betty Grable, but without any make-up. She walked and looked like a film star, and people treated her that way. The people at the Oldham Tabernacle took to her immediately - she was such a contrast to W.P. of the previous year! Maynard insisted she wore a hat, which she did with great reluctance. Like W.P., however, she had an effective word, and her visit brought much encouragement. I still have an old Bible which she endorsed "Love Nettie".

I clearly remember my father's capable handling of these Convention Services, and many others have borne witness to this also. One prominent preacher from outside the holiness movements gave a sermon which was clearly not quite in keeping with the Wesleyan interpretation of Sanctification. I shall never forget Maynard getting up after the address, obviously very unhappy about what had been said. You could hear a pin drop. Very quietly he thanked the speaker for what he had said, but pointed out that the Bible taught a thorough cleansing from sin, and that this is what the C.H.C. and the Easter Convention stood for.

This was typical of Maynard. He never failed to grasp a nettle, and he had great moral courage. His close friend Jack Ford often acted as a restraining influence when Maynard was being merely impetuous; but both were men of outstanding integrity and were never afraid of battling for the truth.

The post-war years also saw the beginning of Maynard's world travels. We have seen that even during the war he visited Eire. These visits were to continue throughout his life, when a visit to Northern Ireland would also include a visit to the South. Usually he went at the invitation of the Irish Evangelistic Band, but openings in Presbyterian and Methodist churches also came his way. The Lord gave Maynard a special anointing in Ireland, and I have met a number of people who have been touched by his ministry there. Principal Herbert McGonigle has commented: *"His influence in Ireland was wide and lasting"*.[8] It was due to Maynard's contacts that I spent a period of study in Dublin, lodging in the home of Miss Celeste Smith, who is a supporter of the Holiness Movement.

Maynard's first major visit abroad was to the United States in the summer of 1947, when he was invited to preach at a number of Church of the Nazarene centres and to take part in the Fourth Quadrennial International Convocation in September. He had a fruitful time visiting and preaching at various centres, until he arrived at Chicago at the beginning of September. His host was Dr Harry Jessop, his predecessor at the Manchester Tabernacle. It was a remarkable Convocation, as Maynard himself has recalled:

"At 8 o'clock that evening (3rd September) the long awaited Convocation began. From that hour until late on Sunday, there were witnessed never-to-be-forgotten scenes of holy power, joy and triumph. It seemed as if the elect of America had gathered for those six days....... Never in all my experience of Convention and Conference gatherings have I witnessed a more beautiful spirit of love, unity, and quiet poise than that which pervaded the Convocation. The stirring singing under the able leadership of Professor Kenneth Wells; the powerful messages from God-anointed preachers; the thought-provoking round-table conferences; the bracing fellowship of saints in dining halls and chapel; the crowded altars with their seeking souls (in one afternoon alone

---

[8] Letter to author, 8th April 1992.

there were about forty seekers) made up a pageant of glory which seemed to ante-date the Millennium itself.[9]

After several other visits to Nazarene centres Maynard returned to the United Kingdom and the C.H.C. at the beginning of October. It had been a memorable visit, and the Church of the Nazarene in America had impressed Maynard immensely. The Holiness groups in this country - even when they were all put together - were very small, whereas the Church of the Nazarene was large, vibrant, and influential. It was one of the fastest growing churches in the United States, and there were excellent colleges and facilities unheard of for holiness students and preachers in the U.K. For the moment Maynard put aside the problems raised by "speaking in tongues", and he did not seem to notice that the Nazarene leaders in America were very much against the Tongues movement. At this stage it appeared to be a non-issue.

In 1949 Maynard visited France, and it was a visit in which I happened to play a small part. A fellow boarder at School was Pierre Roberts. He had been brought up in France where his father was a Pentecostal Pastor. His family had survived the German occupation, although Pastor Roberts had been interned. After the war Pierre came to school in Swansea. In the summer of 1949 I cycled to Northern France, and stayed with Pastor and Mrs Cole, who were C.H.C. missionaries in France, living in Paris. I took the opportunity of visiting Pierre, and had the joy of meeting his remarkable parents. Pastor Roberts sounded like a real Welshman when he spoke in English, but his French was perfect and he was often mistaken for a Frenchman. Mrs Roberts, however, sounded like a Welshwoman when she spoke French! They were both extremely hospitable, and they asked me to spend a day or two with them at their holiday home on the Normandy coast. Pastor Roberts was very interested in the Holiness Movement, and one evening I was asked to give a talk on the subject. Although only 18 I had studied some of the works of John Wesley and was able to give some sort of description of the teachings of the C.H.C. Pastor Roberts seemed fascinated and said he would very much like to meet my father. A few months later Maynard made his first visit to Paris to make contact with the C.H.C. work in France, and at the same time he took the opportunity of meeting Pastor Roberts. They took to one another immediately. Maynard has written about that visit:

---

[9] Flame, November-December 1947 p.35, 36.

"The Pastor of the flourishing Church in Rue de Musset, Paris, is a Holy Ghost filled Welshman named Roberts. For 25 years he has laboured in France, spending 4 years during the war in an internment camp near Paris. This good brother - who, with his gracious wife, gave me a warm welcome - acted as my interpreter for most of the time. What a splendid interpreter he proved to be! When I shouted he shouted, when I gesticulated he responded perfectly - until we seemed to be one."[10]

The contact was something of an eye-opener. Here were Spirit-filled Christians who had wine on the table. They enjoyed French living and eating, and lingered long over the dinner table. The C.H.C. forbade the drinking of alcohol as a condition of membership, and Maynard often preached against the evils of Drink. After this visit, however, he came to realize that some Christians were able to drink without losing their faith. It was never a position he took himself, and he remained a total abstainer; but I think he became a little more tolerant of others.

HOME LIFE

From 1947 onwards, father figured much more prominently in our home life. First at Uppermill and then at Stalybridge, he was for the first time for many years at home more than he was away. Home life was bound up with the college, but it was not an unpleasant life. Stephen and I became very much involved with the Uppermill Cricket Club, and we even appeared for the 2nd XI, which was quite an honour for two young lads in an area where cricket was almost a religion. At Stalybridge we changed over to tennis, not because we had lost our love for cricket, but because there was a nearby club which had many young members.

This is the period when there was real tension between two life-styles. Stephen and I were growing up and I was at University. All our friends at the tennis club went to the cinema and attended local hops (dances). We wanted to try out these activities but were strictly forbidden by our parents. I am afraid we resorted to deviousness, and often pretended we were going to a friend's house, when in fact we were going to a dance or the pictures. In any case we had to hurry home, as father got very annoyed if we were out after 10 o'clock. Some years later, when Kenneth was in his teens, our parents seemed far less strict. Perhaps they had decided they were on the losing side! Whatever

---

[10] Flame, January-February 1950 p.33.

the reason, Kenneth had a far easier time. It is easy to condemn them for being too strict, and at times it did feel like a straight-jacket. I remember one occasion when father arrived at a party where we were dancing. He came up to me in the middle of the dance and asked me to return home with him. I was about 18 at the time, but meekly followed him home. However, looking back I realize they were merely following their convictions. They had made a clean break with the "world", which they regarded as exceedingly harmful, and they had no choice but to bring up their children in the way they believed right. It was narrow and we did rebel; and, like many children brought up in the holiness movement, we did not continue as members when we grew older. But I do not regret my upbringing; there were far more pluses than minuses. Father took a great interest in our university careers and the subjects we were studying. My main subject was history, and, a little later on, theology; and he was fascinated by both subjects. He had a good mind, and was well read in some areas. We spent many hours discussing Oliver Cromwell and George Fox.

Another plus was friendship with Jack Ford, or Mr Ford as we always called him in those days. (He was, of course, to become "Dr. Ford".) He was tutor of Church History at the College and became Pastor of the Ashton-u-Lyne Church. We got to know him well and admired him tremendously. He often came swimming with Stephen and me, and always took an interest in what we were doing. Somehow he was more "earthed" than our own parents. He was interested in sport, cars, and motor bikes! In spite of being such a busy man - amongst other things he took university degrees by correspondence - he always had time for us.

I think mother found life trying at times. Being a Principal's wife in a small college meant a lot of hard work. She had to take on a great deal of responsibility and work, often stooping to scrub floors, as well as bring up her own family. The frustration was largely suppressed, and she continued to be a very loving person, but looking back I can see the nervous strain she was often under.

One point where home, college, and community met was at the Friday night meeting to which I have already referred. We were always encouraged to attend, and generally speaking we thoroughly enjoyed the vibrant atmosphere. Mother nearly always sparkled on these occasions.

By 1950, when Maynard resigned, in order to free himself for evangelistic work, the College appeared to be a on a firm foundation. He was handing over to his friend Jack Ford, who had established himself as an able scholar. There were sixteen students, and the scene seemed set for expansion.

There were, however, many tensions in other parts of the movement. By 1950 the Missionary work overseas was facing great difficulty. Clifford and Elenor Filer had been unable to obtain re-entry permits to return to Colombia, although they did manage to obtain one the following year. Some of the missionaries were not very well and under some strain. At home the very able missionary secretary, George Deakin, became drawn to the Pentecostal Movement, and left the C.H.C. in 1949. And then there were added financial problems, which at times meant it was very difficult to find the money to pay the missionaries.

It was also becoming clear that Leonard Ravenhill was very restless in the C.H.C. He had no quarrel with Maynard or with the Movement which he had helped to found - I think he just needed a wider sphere of work, which he was to find in U.S.A. However he did not actually resign until 1951.

It was a difficult time for Maynard and his colleagues. Jack Ford has written about Maynard's dilemma during the period leading up to 1950:

"No-one felt the tensions of this period more than James. Extension was part of his nature, and anything approaching withdrawal or a mere maintenance of the status quo gave him deep concern. To add to his burden his leadership came under question by some. James, like most religious leaders of the charismatic type, had a strain of mysticism. 'Signs' and 'Seals' and inward impressions as well as providential circumstances all played a part in his attempt to discern the will of God..... He deplored the excessive time spent in Executive meetings, and there are repeated references in the Minutes of this period to his late arrival and his departure before the close."[11]

But Jack Ford went on to acknowledge that it is possible to exaggerate the frustrations. There were very many encouragements including the continuing success of the Flame and the wonderful response that Maynard was receiving on his evangelistic tours. By 1950 both Maynard and the Calvary Holiness Church stood at the crossroads. The next five years would be crucial.

---

[11] S.J.W. p.164.

20. *Maynard and Louie
with Pastor and
Mrs Roberts in Paris.*

21. <u>*Staff and Students at Beech Lawn College*</u>

*Seated l-r Rev. Percy Hassam, Pastor James Taylor, Rev. Jack Ford, Maynard,
Louie, Rev. Clifford Filer and Rev. Harold Hawkins.*

CHAPTER ELEVEN

A WORLD-WIDE MINISTRY

The late Forties had seen the beginning of Maynard's wider ministry. The Fifties were to record an increase in his travel and to realize some rewarding opportunities to preach the gospel of full salvation.

It would be tedious to record all the campaigns of those challenging years, so we shall merely attempt to pick out a few highlights. However, to readers who have been touched by unnamed campaigns I offer my apologies, for wherever Maynard went lives were changed. This was, of course, the work of the Holy Spirit, but the Holy Spirit needs human channels and Maynard's prayer life and single-mindedness were God's opportunity.

In May 1951, Maynard left Britain for his second visit to the United States. After several campaigns he visited California in September. He wrote at the time:

"I am having one of the most wonderful times of my life. Up to the time of writing there have been about 130 seekers at the altar in this place, and I am expecting another break in the final service tomorrow."[1]

From Pasedena he went to Alhambra and Long Beach; and in early November he flew to Texas where he held a few services. Then on 12th November 1951 he began the most interesting, although at times frustrating, part of his journey. He flew to Havanna the capital of Cuba, where he stayed for a week with Pastor Lyle Prescott, Superintendent of the Church of Nazarene in Cuba. He preached at eight mission churches, speaking through an interpreter to *"people who had not grasped the elements of real Christian experience."*[2]

Pastor Prescott's home was badly robbed during his stay, and Maynard marvelled at the courage and faith of the missionaries who followed God's call in such difficult circumstances.

It was while he was at Havanna that the long-awaited visa to Colombia was forthcoming. I remember father telling us of his time at the Colombian Legation. The official was still in bed at mid-day but in the afternoon Maynard managed to see him and thankfully received the required document. On 19th November Maynard flew to Baranquilla in Colombia, where he was met by

---

[1] Flame, November-December 1951 p.29.

[2] Flame, January-February 1952 p.17.

Clifford Filer; and from there they both flew to C.H.C. headquarters at Bogata.

I have already mentioned the problems that the Movement was facing regarding missionary work in Colombia. Maynard was now able to make an assessment himself; and he soon came to realize just how difficult the situation was. The climate itself was extremely trying, being one of the worst parts of the tropical belt. But a bigger problem was Roman Catholic opposition. For example, walking down the streets of Santa Marta Maynard came across such notices as: *"Protestants take notice. We are Catholics. Do not enter this home. We do not want your propaganda."* A picture of the Virgin was accompanied by a prayer asking for protection against Protestant propaganda![3]

Then there was roaring inflation which made the work of the missionaries even more expensive. Maynard estimated that the C.H.C. needed to increase its giving to Colombia threefold in order to maintain the work. This was soon to prove too great a task, and the C.H.C. gradually withdrew from Colombia. However, at this stage Maynard was intensely moved by what he had seen, and pleaded for more money and prayer for the work to continue.[4]

Maynard was back in the U.K. in time for a Week of Prayer and Fasting, commencing on 6th January 1952. It was the beginning of a momentous year in the life of the nation, for it was the year in which George VI died. Maynard wrote of this event in the March-April Flame:

"The passing of George VI had a mysterious prescience. It was as if God had suddenly hushed the turbulent spirits of millions of busy mortals, that He might speak of soon-coming events. One sensed the closing of an epoch and heard the warning note of advancing forces which would test the Empire to its very depths. Death brought a pause that men might prepare."

Maynard could hardly have foreseen that within a decade the Empire would be crumbling, but he certainly had a foreboding.

Maynard was soon away on his round of C.H.C. Churches and within six weeks of his return had visited nineteen centres, and had covered the entire C.H.C. circuit by the middle of March. His life was one of intense activity, and yet backed up by constant prayer.

---

[3] Flame, January-February 1952, p. 19.

[4] Flame, March-April 1952, p. 16.

In the summer of 1952 he visited France, and again made contact with the Coles and with Pastor Roberts. I think it was through the latter that there came the chance of a visit to Bex in Switzerland for an international Convention with speakers from several denominations. Maynard records his joy at being able to preach "entire sanctification" at this important gathering.[5]

And so the days went by with writing, travelling, and a certain amount of administration, as he was still President of the Calvary Holiness Church. While he realized the importance of administration, and he certainly wanted to have a major say in important decisions, he found a lot of committee work an imposition on time that could be given to prayer, study, and evangelism.

It must have been about this time that Maynard came to know Duncan Campbell, the prophet to the Hebrides. In the autumn and winter of 1949 a wonderful revival broke out in Lewis and the surrounding islands. It was hardly noticed at the time by the Christian Church in England or elsewhere. The first time that most holiness folk heard about it was probably from a short report in the Flame in the September 1950. This was followed by a much fuller account in January 1951, with an article by the Rev. Duncan Campbell, who had been mightily used by God as a leader in the revival. He shrank from the term "leader", as he wished to give all the praise to the Lord. He believed in the blessing of holiness and was invited to preach for the Calvary Holiness Church. I think his first appearance was at the Sheffield Convention in September, 1953. Maynard was in Scotland at the time, but it was the beginning of a close association with the holiness folk and with Maynard in particular. It was a friendship which Maynard treasured.

But while a new friendship was being formed with an outstanding man of God, another spiritual giant completed his earthly pilgrimage. On Thursday, 15th January 1953, Mr J.D. Drysdale, the founder of Emmanuel Bible College, Birkenhead, died quietly in his sleep at the age of 73. Maynard had known him for many years, and a number of C.H.C. pastors and missionaries had been trained at the College. The funeral was a service of triumph. Both Maynard and Jack Ford took part and one who was present recorded these words about Maynard's contribution, which was typical of so many of his moving prayers:

---

[5] Flame, July-August 1952, p.33.

"The Rev. Maynard James, President of the Calvary Holiness Church, prayed. His prayer contained everything that was necessary to make this into the kind of service that Mr Drysdale would have himself desired it to be; there was rejoicing at the certainty of God's eternal existence and the wisdom of His purposes for us; there was the praise for the blessing, fruitage, and inspiration of the life that was ended; there was reiteration of the doctrine for which he had so faithfully and earnestly contended; and there was above all a definite note of challenge to all who were intently listening."[6]

The year 1953 was a crucial one for me personally and Maynard's role was significant. I had completed a degree in history and was taking a further degree in theology at Cambridge University. But I was in turmoil. The course was being financed by the Church of England, by whom I had been accepted as a candidate for the ministry. I was, however, a very reluctant ordinand. I felt somehow trapped, and very much wished that I had not agreed to the course.

During the Easter holidays I got into a terrible state about it, and felt I must somehow withdraw from both the degree and the obligation. Now Maynard must have been disappointed that I had not in the first place applied to the Calvary Holiness Church for training and ordination. It was the Church which he had helped to found and which had seen the mighty hand of God's blessing. Moreover, he did not agree with the practice of Infant Baptism in the Church of England. And yet he had not in any way opposed my quest for another denomination, and he had expressed joy when I was accepted for ordination. But now all was in the melting pot. It would have been a good opportunity for him to have tried to make me change to the C.H.C. track. Instead he asked me very quietly: "Paul, are you willing for God's will in this matter?" It was one of the most searching questions I have ever faced, and it was indeed a turning point in my life. When I finally said I was willing, we prayed together and asked the Lord to make his purposes perfectly clear. The prayer was answered in a remarkably short time. I went to see the Secretary of the Anglican Board of Ministry, Prebendary Philip Wheeldon (later Bishop Wheeldon), and told him of my uncertainties. He replied: *"Paul, I'm sure God is calling you to ministry in the Church of England; but go back to your studies in Cambridge without any sense of obligation, and use the money we are giving*

[6] J.D.Drysdale - Prophet of Holiness, by Norman Grubb, p.250, 251.

you. *If at the end of the degree course you are still uncertain of your vocation we shall not ask you to return the money."* There were also other clear indications that God was asking me to go ahead. The doubts soon vanished, and I knew God had called me to serve him in this way. But without my father's gracious intervention I might well have left Cambridge and the Church of England.

In the autumn of 1953 Maynard undertook his very first visit to South Africa, a country which he came to love very much and to defend against many critics. It was a memorable journey. His itinerary was arranged by the African Evangelistic Band, an interdenominational Holiness movement in Southern Africa. He was met at Cape Town by three well known Christian leaders: Captain G.S. Dobbie, Principal of the Glenvar Bible School, H.G. Semark, the Superintendent of the A.E.B., and A.J. Rowlands, who made it his duty to welcome as many missionaries as he could when they landed at the Cape. He was an amazing character who had known Ghandi and Rhodes personally; and had done valiant work for the Master over many years.

Maynard preached at many centres throughout South Africa, including the Glenvar Bible School, before he took part in the A.E.B. Convention at Durban in November. But perhaps the most exciting events were those that have not been formally recorded. I believe it was on this visit that Roger Voke entered into an experience of sanctification through Maynard's preaching and Roger himself has since had a powerful ministry. When I myself visited the Cape in 1984 I heard a Cape-coloured pastor testify to the fact that he had come to the Lord through the ministry of Maynard during that first visit. He was, in 1984, the pastor of a vigorous congregation.

One incident which has been recorded, however, took place on a railway journey to Durban. In Maynard's own words: *"For most of my long journey my only companion was a railway employee setting out on a brief holiday. An addict to liquor he soon brought out his spirit flask.......... Later in the journey there came in a passenger who seemed on the verge of suicide or murder. He too was a slave to strong drink. Frankly he told of his downfall and domestic misery. Presently all three of us dropped on our knees in the compartment. As I prayed for this desperate man, tears came to his eyes and he was visibly moved by the Holy Spirit. In a few*

*days time he obtained work and invited me to his home....... I have
faith that one day he will find the Saviour.*"[7]

There were many happy contacts during Maynard's long stay in
Southern Africa, including a happy reunion with the Rev. Derek
Pass and his wife Olwen. Derek, like his father, had worked as
a C.H.C. pastor in England but was now a minister at Springs
Baptist Church.

The highlight of the whole journey was Maynard's visit to
Swaziland where the I.H.M. had pioneered in a remarkable way.
The I.H.M. was now joined to the Church of the Nazarene (*see
next chapter*), and the work continued to prosper. Maynard had
a joyful reunion with Kenneth Bedwell, who had been working in
Swaziland for many years. Kenneth had been on that very first
trek with Maynard and they had remained firm friends. The
friendship was remarkable when we consider the great distance
in miles between them at a time when travel was much more
difficult than it is today and also the rift that had existed
between the C.H.C. and I.H.M. Kenneth Bedwell was now a
stalwart of the work in Swaziland. The I.H.M. (now the Church
of the Nazarene) had made a big impact in Swaziland. I have
met an Anglican bishop from that country who spoke to me most
glowingly of the work of Dr. David Hynd, a Church of the
Nazarene missionary, who became a national figure and was
honoured by the King of Swaziland. His picture was even put on
a series of Swazi postage stamps! Kenneth was not as well
known as his famous colleague, but nevertheless he was one of
the outstanding missionaries of his time. Maynard has written
of his stay at Stegi with Pastor Bedwell:

*"For five never-to-be-forgotten days I shared in the Conference
gatherings for native pastors, evangelists, and students at this
important Church of the Nazarene Station, covering some 300
acres. The Stegi station comprises a splendid Bible School (of
which Kenneth Bedwell is the Principal), a Dispensary, and a Day
School, and a Church with six outstations and schools."*[8]

Maynard was captivated by the Swazis, especially with their
singing, which was like "the sound of many waters". The last
days of 1953 were with these lovely people, staying at mission
stations with Dr. & Mrs Hynd and other missionaries. Maynard
was moved to the depths of his being:

---

[7] Flame, March-April 1954 p.18.

[8] Flame, March-April 1954 p.20.

"It did not seem possible that in nine short days I would see with my own eyes hundreds of black-skinned men kneel unashamedly in the open and earnestly pray for Christ to fully enter their hearts."[9]

Maynard finished 1953 on a note of great expectancy. He wrote: "Thus 1953 closed with unforgettable memories of wistful, dusky faces, of soul-haunting melodies, and of impassioned prayers from longing hearts..... To win souls at all costs must be my passion for 1954. For soul winning is the greatest vocation in the world......But there is a price to be paid. Souls are not easily won; and the kingdom of darkness will fiercely contest every attempt to rescue men from destruction. O Jesus Christ, Thou great lover of souls, give us Thy compassion, strength, and grace, that we may share with Thee in seeking the lost! Amen."[10]

22. _A Calvary Holiness Church Group_

(Seated from l.) Randolph Murray, Jack Ford, M.G.J., Leonard Ravenhill, Clifford Filer, Herbert Baldwin. (Standing far l.) Harold Hawkins. (Centre bk) Lucy Taylor.

---

[9] Ibid p. 22.

[10] Ibid p. 22.

23. *The James' Family at Beech Lawn College.* (l-r) *Maynard,*
Stephen, Louie, Paul, Kenneth.

CHAPTER TWELVE
THE MOVE TO UNITY

Maynard did not leave South Africa until the end of March 1954, and his remaining weeks were packed with meetings in various parts of that great country, though most of the period was spent in the Johannesburg and Transvaal areas, including a short stay with the Rev. and Mrs C.J. Pass, the parents of Derek, who were now working with the Church of the Nazarene in South Africa. C.J. had been the "committee man" of the C.H.C. and had done much to improve its organization. Now he was Principal of the Nazarene European Training College in South Africa.

Maynard's last campaign was at Pietermaritzburg, Natal. The services were crowded, and into the meeting one night came a student who was studying agriculture. He was an earnest young Christian, and he was greatly moved by Maynard's sermon and came forward at the time of the appeal. Maynard himself counselled him. "What is it you are seeking?" he asked. "I think it is sanctification and the Spirit's Fullness", replied the student. Maynard then quoted 1 Thessalonians 4:3, "This is the will of God, even your sanctification". And he added: "If God wants it for you surely you can believe him to do it." They prayed together and asked God to work mightily in his heart. On the way back to college the student got down in the dust on one of the unmade roads and asked God to fill him with his Spirit. That experience changed his life.[1] His name is Colin Peckham, and in subsequent years he became, like Roger Voke, an outstanding preacher of the Gospel of Full Salvation. He is now Principal of the Faith Mission College in Edinburgh, and he is married to Mary (née Morison).

Maynard returned to a home church that was facing difficulties. The overseas Missionary work was desperately short of cash, and much of the outreach was having to be curtailed. On the home front, the Forward work in raising up new Churches had come almost to a halt; and the College at Beech Lawn, Stalybridge had only five students.

The picture was not totally black, however. Maynard himself was exercising a most fruitful ministry and the Flame magazine was being widely read outside the C.H.C., although its circulation had dropped to 17,000. The well-established centres were

---

[1] Related to author by Rev. Colin Peckham on 1st May 1992.

progressing, but this certainly did not satisfy Maynard. His vision was "Britain for Christ". He was very much encouraged by Dr. Billy Graham's visit to Harringay, and he felt the Holiness Movements could be doing more to preach the Gospel of full salvation.

It had always been the hope of the Four Men, James, Ford, Filer, and Ravenhill, that one day the holiness groups would unite. There were regrets about the 1934 break-away, although Maynard continued to feel that the split had been inevitable at the time. As we have seen the International Holiness Mission from which the Four had originally come was now united to the Church of the Nazarene, thus making it a part of a worldwide fellowship. A leading figure in the movement towards unity was the Rev. J.B. Maclagan. He had been Minister of Parkhead Nazarene Church in Glasgow, and had then moved to the I.H.M. Tabernacle in Battersea. He worked incessantly for union between the two bodies, and this was achieved in 1952.[2]

J.B. Maclagan was a close friend of both Maynard and Jack Ford. At this period I was at Cambridge University and formed a very warm friendship with J.B.'s elder son, David, who was a fellow student.[3] I stayed with David at his home in Battersea, and Mr and Mrs Maclagan were like an uncle and aunt.

Mr Maclagan was very keen that the C.H.C. should also join the Church of the Nazarene, and this must have had some affect on his two friends. Moreover, the Rev. George Frame was Superintendent of the Church of the Nazarene in Britain. He also was a close friend, and a meeting was arranged between the three men - James, Ford, and Frame, at the City Station Hotel, Leeds, on 6th September 1954; and as a result of the discussion Mr Frame (later Dr. Frame) was invited to meet the C.H.C. Executive Council in Ashton-under-Lyne the following day. This led to a special meeting being called for ministers of the Movement for 27th October in Salford, and to consultations with each C.H.C. centre soon afterwards. Maynard wanted the union to go ahead; and although he had some serious reservations, he felt these could be sorted out; and this is shown by the role he himself took in the movement to full unity.

Not all the pastors were in favour of the merger, especially those with pentecostal leanings. Pastor Stephen Travis was very suspicious and made his feelings known throughout the

---

[2] S.J.W. p.128 - 130.

[3] Now a Church of Scotland Minister.

movement.[4] In view of the unease felt by some of the ministers, Maynard called a meeting of ministers for December 16th at Oldham. Meanwhile he wrote to Superintendent Frame setting out the position of the C.H.C. regarding the gifts of the Spirit. As Dr. Ford has put it: *"It became one of the vital documents relating to union."* It also has a bearing on what was to happen in the 1970's. (see Chapter 18). We give a short extract from that letter, as recorded by Dr. Ford:

"We affirm ... that we are one with the Church of the Nazarene in the glorious doctrine of entire sanctification....

1. *We do **not** believe that speaking in other tongues is the initial evidence of the Baptism of the Holy Spirit.*
2. *We do not deny that there may be a genuine gift of "tongues" in operation today, so we dare not adopt the unscriptural attitude of forbidding to speak in another tongue **provided** we are **sure** it is really of the Holy Spirit...*
3. *We believe that 'speaking in tongues' is the least of the nine gifts.... Time and again it has been found that its unwise use in the church assemblies has led to strife, spiritual pride and division... Therefore we feel, after painful experience, that we cannot encourage our people to speak in other tongues in Church gatherings....*
4. *We believe that the infallible proofs of the spirit-filled life are;*
    a. *Purity of heart (Acts 15:8-9)*
    b. *The fruits of the Spirit (Gal.5: 22-23)*
    c. *Power for effective service for Christ (Acts 1:8)*
5. *If freedom of conscience be given to us on the aforementioned matters, and confidence be reposed to us as ministers of Christ to do all in our power to further the interests of Scriptural Holiness through the agency of the Church of the Nazarene, then we would gladly welcome the fusion of the C.H.C into the Church of the Nazarene and would count it a privilege to serve as ministers in its ranks."*

The meeting on 16th December passed a motion: *"That we go ahead with fusion, providing the question raised by Bro. James's statement be agreed to by the Church of the Nazarene H.Q."* This was carried by seventeen votes for the motion, three against, and four abstentions.

Although Maynard's essential position on the "Gifts" had not changed, he seems to have become more cautious about "tongues".

---

[4] S.J.W. p.170, 171.

It is my own view that if he had been more enthusiastic about the pentecostal movement at this period the move to unity would not have gone forward. As it was the merger nearly broke down because of Church of the Nazarene's reservations about the position stated by Maynard's letter. To rescue the situation, Jack Ford put forward a compromise suggestion:

"We understand that, in welcoming us into the Church of the Nazarene, the authorities give us freedom to hold these convictions although they may not express the official Nazarene attitude."[5]

It was a compromise which had in it the seeds of discontent, and it put the C.H.C. pastors in a difficult position. Maynard never explained to me why he went along with this. I do think he regretted it in later years, but at the time he was overjoyed to join a Church with a world vision. He had seen the Spirit move in the Camp Meetings in the States, and I think he felt the matter would soon resolve itself under the guidance of the Holy Spirit.

The official union took place in the Houldsworth Hall, Manchester, on June 11th 1955. Maynard wrote in his diary:

"Eventful day in my life. Today I cease to be C.H.C. president.... Good company in the Houldsworth Hall. Fine spirit: real sense of God's presence".[6]

The next edition of the Flame had articles about the Union, including an important Editorial by Jack Ford in which he referred to the breach with the I.H.M. in 1934 in rather regretful terms;[7] but they could now look forward to further expansion in Christ's name. As Jack put it:

"The three groups (I.H.M., Church of the Nazarene, and C.H.C.) are now bound together in an international Church..... and (quoting from the Final Delegates' Conference of the C.H.C.) 'We face the future, conscious of the call of God to continue our service in union with our brethren in the Church of the Nazarene, with the confidence that the larger unity will result in more widespread and abiding blessing'."[8]

---

[5] S.J.W. p.13.

[6] 1955 Diary.

[7] It is the author's opinion that Jack Ford came to think that the breach could have been avoided, whereas Maynard thought it had been unfortunate but inevitable.

[8] Flame, July-August 1955 p.33.

While the merger had the overwhelming support of most of the members of the denomination, there were those who were deeply disappointed. One such was Mr Hales from Gillingham. He was a wealthy market gardener who loved both the C.H.C. and Maynard. Dr. Albert Lown has written: *"Bro. Hales recalled - chalk, cherries, cheese; and victoria plums from his orchards."* I did not know Maynard's early benefactors but I did know Mr Hales. He was a truly lovely man, and he had supported the Movement with prayer and finance for many years. To him the C.H.C. was like a godly child. Now it had been taken away. No doubt he finally agreed that the merger had to take place, but even I at the time could see that he was deeply disappointed.

If Maynard had misgivings he was too busy to express them even to himself. He had again taken on the Principalship of Beech Lawn College, although only as a temporary measure, until the College could be united with the Church of the Nazarene College.

The Flame continued, but as time went on it became more and more an independent holiness magazine which had no denominational bounds. Indeed the merger was a great release for Maynard. He was first and foremost an evangelist, and once the temporary job at the College was completed that summer, he was able to become a full-time roving evangelist. Beech Lawn College was closed in order to merge with Hurlet College in Glasgow; (and in 1959 the College was moved to Didsbury, Manchester, where it still continues to flourish).

Mr Norman Grubb has written of that period:

"Then came the time when the Nazarenes seemed to take over and absorb the C.H.C., but I loved the way Maynard gave his ultimatum that he would only remain 'Nazarene' so long as he could remain Maynard of the Holy Spirit, and to preach, teach, and go as God led; and he never moved from that, and so great was their respect for him that they gave him that kind of special licence."[9]

Of course, that is written with hindsight, and it did not seem so clear cut at the time. I do not think Maynard had any intention of becoming a freelance evangelist, but this is more or less what he became, while moving in and out of Nazarene circles quite freely. It would be many years before "tongues" would become an issue again.

---

[9] Letter to author, 2nd June 1988.

Conversely the merger gave Jack Ford much more scope for a settled ministry. His gifts of lecturing and teaching were to be fulfilled at the Nazarene College, where he later became Principal, and where he could enjoy the resources and facilities of the Church of the Nazarene. He clearly enjoyed being part of the larger denomination, and the tongues issue was never as important to him as to Maynard. For example, in his book, *"In the Steps of John Wesley"*, he wrote (page 277) that the 1934 split was not about doctrine but the presentation of doctrine. Maynard in his own copy inserted a question mark in his own handwriting. The move suited both men for quite different reasons, and their work was to develop along rather different lines. However, their friendship remained unimpaired.

We cannot leave this chapter without brief mention of the other two pioneers. Leonard Ravenhill was now pursuing a powerful ministry in the United States which continues to this day. (His preaching now is probably over, because he has suffered a stroke, but his prayer life and influence continue.) His vibrant preaching and writing have had a profound influence, and I heard George Verwer, the founder of Operation Mobilisation, testify to the influence of Leonard Ravenhill upon his own ministry. Clifford Filer, on the other hand, returned to Britain with his family in 1952 after very difficult missionary work in Colombia, South America. With true humility and doggedness he was determined to be a burden to no-one, and for a time took a job as a gardener. However, he was soon to find his true role as a pastor, first at Ashton-u-Lyne, and later at Llay in North Wales. He became much loved as he poured out himself for his people, helped greatly by his wonderful wife, Elenor. Perhaps we could say Leonard and Maynard were prophets and evangelists, Jack was a teacher, and Clifford a pastor. Of course, labels are an over-simplification, and there is often a criss-cross of function. But if you were in trouble you would have found a ready listener in all four, but if you had to choose you probably would have chosen Clifford!

CHAPTER THIRTEEN
A PERIOD OF CHANGE

In the previous chapter we saw the success of the move to unity, and some of the implications of this merger. In the early days, however, it did not seem such a critical change. Maynard was now a Nazarene Minister, and many of his visits were to Nazarene centres, including former I.H.M. and C.H.C. Churches. He was still visiting the same sort of people as he had been visiting in earlier years, and although he was no longer President, his standing was very high in Holiness circles.

Mid-July, 1955, found Maynard in Ardrossan in Scotland for a Convention. It was to be a memorable visit. At the opening meeting he preached on *"The way of Holiness"*, and his diary records four seekers. He phoned Louie that night only to hear that Mr Len Tingle, from the Sheffield Assembly, had been killed by lightning while witnessing at the Ascot Racecourse. Len was a real *"Valiant-for-Truth"* and he went all over the country distributing texts and tracts. The Tingle family were close friends of ours, and Stephen and I knew them well, incl-uding their daughter Dorothy, to whom Stephen was very attached at one time. The news of Len's death was a sad blow.

The Convention at Ardrosson experienced a time of blessing, in spite of the shadow of Len Tingle's death. Indeed it is often the case that God comes to us in special ways when we are feeling at our worst. The Convention continued until 25th July, and Maynard preached the final sermon on *"The Judgement Seat of Christ"*. He recorded in his diary that it was a *"great time"*, and he also went on to say: *"Lesson learned during the Convention - must have more material"*. This was a very revealing remark. After many years in the ministry he could easily have sailed along with old sermons, and Maynard was never afraid to repeat a good sermon. But he was also keen to keep his mind fresh and his congregations alert.

August was spent in Northern Ireland, but in September Maynard returned to Scotland for services in Albany Street Church, Edinburgh; and it was while here that he heard of his mother's serious condition. On 29th September 1955 he travelled to Bargoed, and joined Louie at 2 Cross Street, where Louie was helping to look after his mother. He wrote in his diary that day: *"Found Mama in poor state. Evident signs of the end. Distressed about her mental suffering. Dear Louie's nerves in a bad condition."*

The next few days were difficult, and Maynard's diary again reveals the conflict that was going on: *"My heart heavy because of Mama's mental anxiety"* (30th September); *"Satan fighting hard to bring in a wedge"* (2nd October); and *"Mama existing on sips of water, very distressing"* (4th October). But Maynard's discipline held and we find him editing the Flame even during those trying days.

The Doctor felt that Gwen could linger on in this way for some time, so on 7th October Maynard returned to Scotland for an appointment at Parkhead Church. His sermon on Sunday 9th of October was entitled *"Rejoice in the Lord"* and he was given *"real liberty"*.[10] The meetings continued with great blessing on Monday and Tuesday, but when he returned to his host and hostess on Tuesday night, he received a phone call from Louie to say that his mother had died earlier that day. He wrote in his diary: *"Dear Mama passed away at 4.40 p.m. Very sad because of Mama's sufferings. Went to bed with a heavy heart. Prayed and was comforted by Matthew 12:20, 'The smoking flax He will not quench'"*.

It was typical of Louie that she waited until after the evening meeting to tell Maynard of the sad news. She realized he would have found it difficult to preach so soon after the news, so she thoughtfully waited a few hours. It was just one example of her life-long support and concern for Maynard's ministry.

Maynard, as he said, went to bed with a heavy heart, crying out to the Lord for comfort. During his sleep he had a remarkable dream, which is best told in his own words:

"In my dream I went to the little room where Mama's dead body lay. Gently I pulled back the sheet that covered her dear face. Then to my astonishment and joy I saw that her face was radiant with a heavenly glory. She said distinctly to me: 'I have a most beautiful place in the Kingdom.' That was all. But it banished all my gloom and filled my soul with the peace that passeth all understanding."[11]

Much comforted he stayed on at Glasgow that day and preached at both morning and evening services. The evening address being on *"The Judgement Seat of Christ"* - one of his most frequently preached sermons! The next day, however, he travelled to Bargoed.

---

[10] Diary, 9th October 1955.

[11] From "Dreams and Voices", unpublished.

The Funeral took place on Saturday 15th October, the Service commencing at the little house in Cross Street, and then moving to the Holiness Mission where Gwen had worshipped for so many years. Maynard wrote in his diary:

"Wonderful Service in the Mission....Brother Jones prayed, splendid word by Brother Williams,[12] followed by a fine word by Jack (Ford). Proceeded to Hengoed Church Yard. Dear Mama's remains were laid to rest alongside those of dear Dada. God's own seal on this eventful day."[13]

After attending to several items of business and visiting friends and relatives over the weekend, Maynard and Louie left Bargoed on Tuesday, 18th October, parting company at Crewe, with Louie returning home to Stalybridge, and Maynard resuming his ministry in Glasgow. But the memories of those days were to remain with him throughout the rest of his life. His mother had brought up him and brother Willie almost single- handed. Her faith had carried her through thick and thin. She had been a shining example of Christian holiness in the Bargoed area, not only by her words but more especially by her life. In spite of the dream Maynard found it difficult to understand why she was so distressed in mind during her last few weeks on earth. The distress of body he could accept, but the other was much harder to comprehend. Should not the Lord give peace to his children at these times? It was a problem he was to grapple with for many years until it was fully worked out in his own experience.

This is probably a good opportunity to say a few words about other members of Maynard's family and relatives at this time. The funeral was indeed a gathering of the clan! His brother Willie was still living at nearby Newport with his wife Emily and son David, who was studying dentistry at Bristol University. (David later practised as a dentist, but eventually took a medical degree, and has become a consultant surgeon in some leading London hospitals.) Stephen and I were both doing our National Service - Stephen as an R.A.F. pilot, and myself as an Army 2nd lieutenant, both of us having completed our degrees at university. Kenneth was still a pupil at Oldham Hulme Grammar School. We all came together for Grandma James's funeral, a truly great family reunion.

We have never visited Bargoed together since the funeral, and I have only been back very occasionally. However, that little

---

[12] William Williams, a stalwart of the Bargoed Mission, see p.74.

[13] Diary, 15.10.55.

home in Cross Street has left its impression on us all. It reminds us of a truly courageous lady, who lived through some very difficult times. She never had much money - at times she had practically none at all - but she won through with faith and grit.

With the family growing up Louie was now much more free to accompany Maynard on his travels. She did indeed go with him abroad on a number of journeys, but she was always pleased to return home! On many other occasions she stayed at home, following the meetings with prayer and telephone calls. "Home", however, was three different places in as many years. At the time of the funeral Louie and Maynard were still living in the grounds of Beech Lawn College, although it was no longer training men for the ministry. The following year they moved to Rose Cottage in Ashton-u-Lyne, but in 1957 they moved to College Road, Oldham, where they stayed until 1963.

After completing his Mission in Glasgow, Maynard visited Bolton and Darlington; and then travelled to Northern Ireland. It would be tedious to give a complete travelogue during the next few months and years. One can only comment that as the years went by he received invitations from as many Churches outside his denomination as he did from the Church of the Nazarene itself. This posed a financial problem. He was being paid as a minister of the Church of the Nazarene but he was also receiving money from the other Churches he visited, especially in the U.S.A. and South Africa. Wages in the C.H.C. had been very low; and in the early 1950's it was about £350 p.a., which was poor pay even in those days; and in the Nazarene Church it was only slightly better. Financially it would have paid Maynard to have free-lanced, but he always gave the Church the monies he had received on his travels, allowing of course for expenses. He believed the labourer was worthy of his hire, but to make a profit never entered his head.

One highlight of 1956 was the visit to the U.S.A. for the General Assembly of the Church of the Nazarene. Maynard and Louie sailed from Liverpool on "The Empress of Britain". I remember it clearly, because Glenys - my fiancée - and I saw them off! It was a rough voyage, and Louie became so sea-sick that the Doctor was called and an injection given. The weather improved, however, and this found Maynard up on deck writing articles for the Flame and also witnessing for the Lord in conversations with other passengers. After arrival at Montreal and some sight-seeing in Canada, including the Niagara Falls, and two or three preachments, they commenced the long two day journey by car to Kansas City.

There were 12,000 present at the Assembly, with delegates from various parts of the world. Both Maynard and Louie found it a moving experience, and they felt very much part of a world-wide fellowship. After the Assembly Maynard commenced a preaching tour before returning to Britain in September, Louie actually leaving a little earlier.

The Fifties rolled on in this way, and we can only pick out a few highlights. The Flame's circulation grew to 20,000, and Maynard continued to contribute stirring and sometimes controv-ersial articles; and at a later point we shall examine some of these controversies. However, his main emphasis was always on Scriptural Holiness, and on this he never wavered. The Editorial Board during these years included the Rev. David Tarrant, who proved to be a very able deputy, especially when Maynard was abroad.

Maynard returned to the United States in 1958, and it is worth recording Maynard's own description of the latter part of that tour: *"The Lord gave us a touch of revival at Minneapolis. Night after night, without any undue pressure in the appeal, souls made their way to the altar, seeking with all their heart the blessing they needed... While in Minneapolis I had sweet fellowship with my dear friend and former colleague, Brother Ravenhill.* [14] *He and his wife, along with the children are now living at the Bethany Fellowship, some twenty miles out of the centre of the city. I told Brother Ravenhill that I wished he were with us in the world-wide fellowship of the Church of the Nazarene.*

"I found at Eastern Nazarene College a band of consecrated tutors, under the humble and efficient leadership of Dr. Edward Mann.... As never before I realize the vital importance of our Nazarene Colleges and Seminary. Satan hates such institutions and will do his utmost to wreck their usefulness in the Kingdom of God.

"Tuesday night November 25th, saw me safely in England again, and the following morning witnessed a glad reunion with my dear wife... I sometimes get tired of travelling so much away from home and loved ones; but the sense of commission is so strong and the time for working in the needy fields of earth is so short - and the sweet presence of our adorable Lord is so real -

---

[14] One of the four founders of the C.H.C, and now working in U.S.A. where he still remains - the only living survivor of the Four.

*that everything outside the task of soulwinning pales into
insignificance alongside the glory of such a vocation.*

> *'To serve the present age,*
> *My calling to fulfil,*
> *O may it all my powers engage,*
> *To do my Master's will!'"*[15]

Almost immediately after his return he was preparing for his
second visit to South Africa, and on Christmas Eve, 1958, he and
Louie sailed from Southampton to Capetown. It was the longest
of all his journeys and one that was rich in blessing. Indeed, the
blessing began on board the ship. They called on a Sunday at
Las Palmas. But let Maynard tell the story:

*"Not only was there no Divine Service that day, but to make
matters worse, the ship was thrown open for the buying of merch-
andise from the traders who came aboard, and for dancing. This
was more than I could stand; so permission was secured from the
Purser to conduct a series of morning Bible studies in the library
and to hold a Gospel service on deck on the following Sunday
evening. The Lord set his seal upon these simple efforts."*[16]

There were services on arrival at Capetown, followed by the
annual A.E.B. Convention at "Glenvar", Kenilworth. It was at
Kenilworth that Maynard wrote:

*"South Africa is ripe for harvest of souls before the inevitable
'blood bath' begins. The whole continent of Africa is like a giant
awakening out of the sleep of ages. Deep-seated fear is gripping
the hearts of many Europeans in beautiful South Africa. No
political expedient can solve the problem. We must pray, fast,
work hard, preach Full Salvation and the Second Coming of
Christ, and believe for a real outpouring of the Holy Ghost before
judgments fall. Please stand with us in prevailing prayer in these
coming months in South Africa."*[17]

Maynard has sometimes been accused of being reactionary, and
we shall examine his political views in a later chapter. However,
we can see from the above quotation that he had a far clearer
perception than most of what was happening in Africa. This was
before Macmillan's *"Wind of Change"* speech which alerted the
world to the changing situation as well as hastening the process
by his very words.

---

[15] Flame, January-February 1959, p.21.

[16] Flame, March-April p.17.

[17] Ibid, p.18.

But to return to Maynard's journey. In late January 1959 Maynard and Louie visited the Second Advent Convention in Johannesburg, where there were record crowds and a large number of seekers for "*entire sanctification*". In early February Maynard led a Tent campaign in Steenberg, and in late February a campaign at Battswood Baptist Church at which there were 120 seekers. In March there were campaigns in Athlone and Capetown, including one at the Docks Mission.

And so it went on throughout the whole of 1959, and on to the March of 1960, although Louie returned home in September 1959. Maynard preached in many parts of that vast country, and also paid another visit to Swaziland.

At the end of March, Maynard left South Africa for Nyasaland, now Malawi, where he attempted to see Dr Banda who had just been released from prison. He did not succeed at the time but a few days later on his flight to Nairobi he found himself sitting next to the future leader of Malawi. Maynard has recounted the conversation:

*"He was en route for London, after his prison release. Small in stature and of a kindly appearance, he willingly talked with me on the long journey. When I asked him if he had ever accepted Jesus Christ as his personal Saviour, he gave an evasive reply: "I would not be an elder of the Church of Scotland unless I had." Later he added: "I am a Christian". When I expressed my concern that his followers hailed him as their 'Messiah' and asked him what it really meant, he said that the title had no religious significance. He was their **political** Messiah, to deliver his people from Colonial domination. He was not a mystic like Ghandhi.*

To my surprise, Dr Banda seemed well-informed on the great Evangelical Revival of the 18th century, and praised the work of Wesley and Whitefield....... when I outlined the policy of our Church of the Nazarene in Nyasaland - that of simply preaching the Gospel of Jesus Christ, and of non-interference in the political affairs of that country - Dr. Banda seemed pleased. As politely as possible I told him that God had allowed him to wield such influence over the Nyasas, his responsibility was great. He could bring blessing or bane to his people. One day we must all stand before God. I promised to pray for him. He thanked me graciously."[18]

On his arrival at Nairobi Maynard met with several Christian groups, and stayed in the home of Dr. Calcott, F.R.C.S. a

---

[18] Flame, May-June 1960 p.28.

prominent eye-surgeon. He then flew on to Jerusalem, attending the Easter morning service at the Garden Tomb. He was very moved by this experience and became determined to take Louie to Israel one day.

He arrived home on Thursday 21st April 1960, and his diary records "*A quiet evening*"! But he was away the next day for meetings at Bolton. There was little rest for this doughty warrior!

24. *Maynard on campaign with musician and evangelist Harry Briggs.*

CHAPTER FOURTEEN
THE SWINGING SIXTIES

The 1960's were a period of great change in the life of the nation. Many people openly abandoned religion; and it was certainly a time when moral standards were lowered. The early Sixties also saw the continued break-up of the British Empire, and even the breakdown of close relations between Britain and South Africa.

The decade began quietly enough for Maynard. After his return from South Africa in April 1960 he undertook several engagements in Britain, and even managed a little time with his family. While he had been abroad Stephen had married Marjorie, and Glenys and I had our first child, Ruth. During the spring and early summer Maynard visited both homes, coming down to Newhaven (where I was a Curate) in May. Maynard wrote in his diary: "*Lovely day with Paul, Glenys, and little Ruth. Went to Brighton in the afternoon. Ruth took to me. Delighted.*" It was indeed a happy day, and he thoroughly enjoyed being a grandfather for the first time.

Soon, however, he was travelling abroad again, and at the end of June he flew to the United States. His first assignment was as a main preacher at the North Reading Camp - one of the great camp gatherings so popular in the States. Other engagements followed, but his main task was to deliver the Heinmuller Lectures at the Kansas Theological Seminary on "*The Devotional Life of the Minister*". He was well fitted to tackle this subject; his busy life was soaked in prayer and the lectures reflected this.

Some of the material was later used for his little book "*When Thou Prayest*", but the bulk of these memorable addresses remain unpublished. We shall give just an extract, so that our readers can get at least the flavour of these lectures.

"*The man who knows how to weep is irresistible. Nothing can turn him from his quest. Ecclesiastical honours, wordly comforts, and financial blandishments are powerless to move his tear-stained heart. He must win souls or die. Such a man is a paradox to unbelievers and carnal Christians. For in spite of his sorrow he is seen to rejoice with exceeding joy. The man who is in the secret place of prayer travails with a holy concern for lost souls, and his face shines with heavenly radiance in the place of public testimony. It is recorded of the late Paget Wilkes, that eminent Holiness preacher and missionary, that during those wonderful revival services in Shanghai in 1925, his face was always shining. Doubtless in private prayer he had his seasons of holy weeping: in public he reaped with joy. Paradoxical though it may seem to be, the fact remains that the most joyful and successful Christian ministers are those who, like the apostle Paul, are 'sorrowful, yet always rejoicing'. The main cause of our barren churches and our joyless congregations is a dry-eyed ministry."*[1]

Throughout the lectures he stressed that much of the weakness in the Church is due to lack of time alone with God. He dealt with such subjects as: the Nature of God, the Need of Humanity, and the Nearness of the Apocalypse. He linked the Perfect Love of God with the experience of Sanctification, whereby we experience the fire of God's love in our own hearts. He emphasized the sinfulness of humanity, and pointed out that *"A sad and sinful world will never come to Christ except as He is made known to them by the Spirit-baptized lovers of the risen Lord."* He castigated those ministers who preached movingly on the Lord's First Coming but totally ignored the promise of His Second Coming. Finally Maynard listed the aids to the Devotional Life as: Private Prayer, the Practice of Fasting, the Reading of Scripture, the Avoidance of a legalistic spirit, and a Spirit of Praise.

All these points were exemplified in his own life. The previous year he had read through the whole Bible, and several parts he had read several times. On the busiest of journeys there was always time for prayer; and one day a week was set aside for fasting, even when he was preaching and lecturing. To review Maynard's sermons and writings without realizing this is to miss the main point.

It seems that the lectures were well received and were the occasion of real blessing. His diary records that he had *"liberty"* throughout the lectures, and after the last one: *"unction"*.

Maynard returned to England in late November 1960, and a few days later he and Louie travelled down to London to support Glenys, Ruth and myself as we sailed for Kenya in East Africa, to serve with the Church in that developing country. It was while we were working in Kenya that our son Adrian, and Maynard and Louie's first grandson, was born.[2]

Maynard rarely wasted a journey. He arranged the send off at King George V Dock to be combined with a preaching weekend in London, and Sunday, 4th December, 1960, found him preaching

---

[1] From Lecture Two, the Heinmuller Lectures, unpublished.

[2] We served in Kenya until June 1965.

both morning and evening at Speke Hall, where so much "*holiness*" work had been pioneered earlier in the century.

Before the year was out, he had travelled to Northern Ireland. We have not given much space to Maynard's visits to Northern Ireland, but they were frequent and fruitful. When he arrived there at the end of the year, it was to a remarkable situation. At the end of 1959 Frank Marshall, the leader of the Irish Evangelistic Band, had begun a campaign in the Ballyrobert Mission Hall, about eight miles from Belfast. The series of meetings was meant to last a fortnight but they went on for 43 weeks! Frank Marshall, like Maynard, was a prayer-warrior, and the campaign was soaked in prayer. The heavenly singing which had been heard in the Hebrides Revival was also heard in Ballyrobert, and Duncan Campell, the prophet to the Hebrides, has said that the blessing in Ballyrobert was the nearest he had experienced to the blessing in the Hebrides.[3]

When Maynard arrived in Northern Ireland the campaign was over, so he had no direct link with it. However, he had previously done a great deal to encourage Frank Marshall, W.T. McClintock and other leaders of the I.E.B. He had preached at their conventions and had stayed in their homes. When Maynard was holding services at Limavady, near Londonderry, in January 1961 Frank Marshall attended some of the meetings, and they had sweet fellowship together.

Maynard's visits to the United States were interesting and profitable, but one can hardly say that they affected the life of the nation. But his journeys to Northern Ireland and to South Africa seem to have been of a different order. In both places he had tremendous blessing and, what is more, his ministry had a profound influence on some of the evangelical leaders in those two countries. It would seem that God was using Maynard as one of his instruments in preparing both countries for their Gethsemanes ahead.

After the encouraging time at Limavady in January, he visited Northern Ireland again in April, being met at the airport by Frank Marshall, with whom he spent most of the day. He had come for a campaign at Ballymena, and he was accompanied by Harry Briggs, a brilliant musician as well as an able pastor and evangelist, who, as we have previously seen, had made an important contribution to the life of the former Calvary Holiness Church. The Ballymena Campaign commenced on Sunday 30th

---

[3] Flame, March-April 1961, p.4,5.

April, and Maynard recorded the day in his diary: "*A wonderful beginning. Praise God!*" Most days he put "*liberty*" in his diary, and on the last day of the campaign, 17th May, he wrote "*Great Liberty*".

The ministry was rather different from the Thirties when new churches were being established. In Northern Ireland he worked either on an inter-denominational basis, usually in association with the I.E.B., or Faith Mission, but he also visited congregations by invitation. But his influence was felt in many parts of the Province, and the Flame became widely read.

He was back there in November, this time for a campaign at Portadown, and again there was much blessing. After the last meeting on 10th December Maynard wrote in his diary: "*Solemn power in preaching on 'The Unpardonable sin'. About 20 seekers. Wonderful seal to last meeting of campaign.*"

The following year 1962 was again filled with constant travel, and if we skip over those journeys it is not because they were unimportant, but simply because outwardly these would seem to be a repetition of what we have previously reported. To those concerned they were, however, of vital importance; and were very much part of the persevering ministry to which every true Minister is called.

1963 saw the passing of one of the saints of the former C.H.C., Mr Herbert Hales, who died at the great age of 93. The funeral took place in the Nazarene Church at Gillingham. Jack Ford paid eloquent tribute to his departed friend whom he had known intimately as a man of the soil, a man of Kent, and, above all, a man of God.

Maynard also spoke at the service, including these words:

"*I have met many good and great men in my time, but never have I met a man who excelled Brother Hales in kindness, Christian sympathy, understanding, gentleness and overflowing generosity. When last Sunday I heard of his home call, I dropped on my knees and gave God thanks for every remembrance of a man who had served Him so faithfully and sacrificially, and had meant so much for the cause of Holiness..... But I must confess that even as I praised the Lord for dear Bro. Hales, a pang of grief came to my heart, when I realized that yet another of my precious friends had slipped away.*"

Maynard then went on to make a Gospel challenge. Where is Bro. Hales now? What is his present state? And will we see him again? He concluded his answers to these questions with the positive assertion:

"If we, like Bro.Hales, will receive Jesus as Saviour and Lord, then we can be certain of a reunion with our brother and the other saints who have gone before us."[4]

1963 saw the publication of Maynard's third book: *"When Thou Prayest"*. It was based on his lectures at Kansas Seminary, but was written in a much simpler form. The subject was very dear to his heart, as we have already seen. Dr Ford described the book as a *"Guide book to the golden highway which the author has trodden faithfully and reverently since he first stepped out for Christ."*[5] Dr. Paul Rees wrote the Foreword, and aptly commented: *"It speaks from within the secret place, where its author is so much at home."* It was dedicated to Louie: *"My devoted wife and prayer partner, who has 'tarried by the stuff'."*

The book urged the reader to retreat to the quiet place, and dealt with such problems as guidance and unanswered prayer. On guidance he listed three ways in which it comes to us: through the Bible; through the inner voice of the Holy Spirit; and through Christian friends. These different forms of guidance should be tested against one another. He gave the moving example of a young missionary who was longing to return to India at the beginning of World War II. At last there was a chance of a boat, and he rang up Maynard to ask his advice as a Christian brother. Maynard asked him: *"Have you had a word from the Lord on this matter?"* *"No"* replied the missionary. *"Then hold steady"*, urged Maynard. The young man did not heed the advice and died at sea as his ship was torpedoed. Maynard thought it was a needless death.[6] As to unanswered prayer, he felt that what we sometimes pray is not good for us, and God loves us too much to give in to a foolish request. On the other hand we often fail to receive an answer because of unbelief.

It is a vital little book, long out of print, but full of first-hand experience and sound advice.

[4] From Maynard's unpublished papers.

[5] Flame, November-December p.21.

[6] "When Thou Prayest", American edition, p.20.

25. *Herbert Hales, the grand old man of the Calvary Holiness Church. "I never met a man who excelled him in kindness". (p.116)*

26. *Two old warriors!*
Major Allister Smith
with Maynard.
(see p.123)

CHAPTER FIFTEEN

THE CALL TO SOUTHPORT AND THE SOUTHPORT CONVENTION

Maynard and Louie had lived most of their married life in towns and industrial areas. In the very early Sixties they were living in College Road, Oldham, very close to Oldham Hulme Grammar School where Kenneth had been a pupil.[1] But Kenneth had now left home, and was teaching in Buxton, so there was no need to continue living in the Oldham area. In 1963 Maynard did not go abroad - unless Eire be counted as such - but nevertheless he was away from home for about 200 nights;[2] and this meant that Louie was on her own in Oldham for most of the time, although she did occasionally accompany Maynard on his travels. Both Maynard and Louie had a great liking for Southport. Kenneth had been to preparatory school there, and the family had made several holiday visits to this sea-side town - although the sea was usually miles out! Maynard used to joke that the town was mentioned in the Psalms: "*The sea saw it and fled*" (Psalm 114:3).

They spotted a house in the Hillside part of Southport. It was a pleasant semi-detached house in a nice area, and very near to the famous Birkdale and Hillside golf courses. After a great deal of prayer they decided to buy it. Houses were very cheap at the time, and with their life-savings they found they could buy it outright for about £2,300.[3] They moved into 35 Arundel Road in early December 1963 and this was to be their settled home for nearly twenty years - by far the longest period in any house.

In all major decisions Maynard sought a seal from the Lord. I am not sure what the seal was in this case, but when they moved in he seemed satisfied that they had done the right thing. A few days after the move be began a campaign in Enniskillen, so he hardly gave himself time to settle down. His introspective mind began to worry, and he anguished about the move. Eventually Louie became so concerned that she offered to move again if this is what he felt was right. It was an astonishingly loyal offer. For thirty years Louie had lived in houses dictated by Maynard's work - apart from the spell in Bargoed during the war. At last

---

[1] Stephen had also attended Hulme Grammar School, while I had been a boarder at Emmanuel Grammar School, Swansea.

[2] Estimated from 1963 diary.

[3] I handled some of the correspondence on this, and £2,300 is the figure that sticks in my mind, although the papers have been destroyed.

she had a pleasant house in a town she had chosen on merit. She was already finding a spiritual home in Boundary Street Mission, and yet she offered it all up! Maynard was very touched by this, and in the end became convinced it was God's will for them to stay. In relating this to me some years later, he said that the heaviness he experienced must have been an attack from Satan because of the important spiritual events which were to occur in Southport.

The town had long been the centre of an annual Methodist Convention which Maynard had attended both as a visitor and a speaker. But Maynard felt the need for a Holiness Convention wider than the bounds of Methodism. During July 1963 he had been preaching at the Camp Meetings in Killadeas on the shores of Loch Erne in Northern Ireland. In Maynard's own words:

"The atmosphere of the place was laden with prevailing prayer - four seasons of intercession each day, conducted by outstanding saints, paved the way for mighty preaching in the demonstration of the Holy Spirit..... Yes, there was something different about the Killadeas Camp, and the writer's heart was deeply stirred. Then in the quietness of a small hut came the clear call of God to do something on similar lines on the west coast of Britain.

"At first it seemed that Llangollen, North Wales, was the place for such a revival. But after much prayer and heart searching it was made clear that Southport, Lancashire, was the appointed venue. But we wanted no clash with any other Full Salvation Conferences in that area, so the saints were consulted before the final decision was reached... Convenors of the Southport Methodist Convention gave their blessing to the proposed venture of faith. And a venture of faith it was. It was to be clearly interdenominational and international. Its objective was to spread the message of Bible Holiness as a revival fire throughout the British Isles and beyond."[4]

Just over a year later, on Saturday 5th September 1964, the very first meeting of the Southport International Revival Convention took place in Church Street Methodist Church, as the previously arranged venue was found to be too small for the expected crowds. The Convention lasted until the following Friday, and all the services were well attended. Most of the speakers were from Holiness Churches and included Clifford Filer, one of the original Four; Stanley Banks, son-in-law of Principal Drysdale and a life-long friend of Maynard; Dr Duewell

---

[4] Flame, November-December 1964, p.27.

from India; Mary Morison from the Faith Mission in Scotland; Ken Terhoven from South Africa; W.E. Brewer from Preston; and James Bell from Kent.

A small committee was formed to organize the Convention, which has been held every September, right up to the present day. It reached great heights in the late Sixties and early Seventies, and brought blessings to thousands of visitors, as well as making an impression on Southport itself. Several of the Southport Churches gave it their support, including Christ Church, the large Anglican Church on Lord Street. Indeed, for several years the Convention was held in this fine building. Maynard became close friends with the Vicars of Christ Church, down the years, including Geoffrey Hart, Martin Hunt, and Garth Grinham - all fine men of God.

The speakers at the very first convention were drawn mainly from Holiness circles, but as the years went by Maynard felt constrained to widen the field. He was becoming very impressed with what was happening in the charismatic field. He never agreed with the over-emphasis on the gifts, but nevertheless he recognized that God was doing something special. He was particularly impressed with what was happening in the Church of England - the dry bones were coming alive! He heard of the work of Michael Harper and David Watson and he was determined that men of this calibre should be invited to the Convention.

Not all the committee were convinced, however; and there were some tense meetings when some of Maynard's suggestions were put forward. However, in the end Maynard won the day, and over the years there were several speakers who might be termed *"charismatic"*. One of the first was the late David Watson, who was then Vicar of St. Cuthbert's Church, York. He first came in September 1969. His visit has been recorded in the Flame; and as I was there myself that night I can vouch for its accuracy:

"Tuesday night's service can never be forgotten. It was one of the highlights of the Convention. The closing speaker was the Rev. David Watson. On the previous night he had testified clearly to a 'second crisis' in his life - a baptism of the Holy Ghost which had revolutionised him. On Tuesday evening he gave a masterly address on the vital theme of faith. When the appeal was given there was an immediate response, and over twenty persons walked out openly to the Enquiry room."[5] (David Watson based his

---

[5] Flame, Novovember-December 1969, p.29.

address on Hebrews 11. I remember it clearly because I read the lesson, part of Hebrews 11, at the meeting!)

One outstanding speaker who came to the Convention very early on was Miss Gladys Aylward, the famous missionary to China, about whom a widely acclaimed film has been made. ("Inn of Seventh Happiness" with Ingrid Bergmann.) She spoke at the 1966 Convention, and received headlines in the local paper. In her address at the final service she spoke of the great need for prayer. She accused many Christians of trifling with the faith: *"Just look around you. Most of our churches are empty. We just seem to be playing around with Christianity."*[6] There were many prominent speakers, including Canon Harry Sutton (of the South American Missionary Society), Pastor Arthur Wallis (later to be associated with the Dales Movement); George Verwer (the founder of Operation Mobilisation); Selwyn Hughes (author of *"Every Day with Jesus"*), and Dr. W.R. Davies.[7] They all made a valuable contribution to the Convention, and all of them testified to a radical experience of the Holy Spirit, even if they did not always put it in terms familiar to Holiness folk.

One regular preacher at the Convention was Major Allister Smith, who became a close friend of Maynard. Major Smith was an officer of the Salvation Army, and his home was in South Africa, although the world was his parish. Many pulpits were open to him and he even preached at the Keswick Convention, which was rare for the radical type of holiness preacher. He had a unique style - very forthright but humorous. He wote many articles for the Flame, and one was in the form of a letter to Maynard:

"I hope you will continue to challenge the national evils that are so alarmingly on the increase on both sides of the Atlantic and to sound aloud your clarion call to revival in this midnight hour, when the return of Christ is so imminent... God bless you, dear warrior-editor. Your friends everywhere know something of the fire that burns in your heart. God has made you a prophet for this hour. Long may your trumpet sound from the watchtower."[8]

Allister Smith stirred up many a congregation at the conventions. He challenged and provoked his listeners to be

---

[6] Flame, November-December 1966 p.5.

[7] Dr. W.R. Davies, a leading Methodist Minister, writer of the foreword of this book, and currently Principal of Cliff College.

[8] Flame, May, June 1964, p.27.

doers as well as hearers. For example, he gave the main message at the Opening Rally in 1976. The Flame reported:

"The closing message was given by that veteran soul winner and hero of a thousand battles - Major Allister Smith. His theme was Revival; and in his inimitable way he set forth the nature and requirements of true revival."[9]

On the Tuesday evening of the same Convention he *"testified of the way God had met with him, saving and sanctifying his soul and empowering him for victorious service. A one-time magistrate he obeyed the call to be a Salvation Army Officer. The sense of presence was so amazing during the Major's testimony that Maynard James could do no other than make brief appeal to those who wanted to be filled with the Holy Spirit to come right out to the altar. Immediately 13 persons walked out to the chancel steps. It was a moving sight to see the old warrior*[10] *put his hands upon the heads of these earnest seekers and pray aloud for their sanctification. Mair Perkins was in tears as she arose to sing another of Zion's sweet songs."*[11]

Mrs Mair Perkins played a inspiring part in a number of the conventions. Her beautiful voice was dedicated to the Lord, and the Holy Spirit spoke through her songs in a powerful way. She came from South Wales, and she and Louie were very close.

Dr Paul Rees was another great favourite at the Convention, although he made only two visits, in 1967 and 1978. He and Maynard had been close friends in the Thirties, [12] and although most of Paul Rees's ministry had been in the States they had kept in close touch. Dr Rees became very well known because of his close association with Billy Graham and his "Lectures for Ministers" at the Westminster Chapel. He had also led the Bible Readings at the Keswick Convention. He gave the Bible Readings at the 1967 Southport Convention, based on Ephesians 5:8, *"For ye were sometimes darkness, but now are ye light..... walk as children of light"* The addresses were wonderfully blessed, and the Flame recorded that at the close of one Bible Reading *"the fragrant presence of the Lord was so evident that seeking souls were invited to enter into their heritage in Christ.....*

---

[9] Flame, November-December 1976 p.28.

[10] It is not clear whether this refers to Maynard or the Major - old warriors both!.

[11] Ibid p.29.

[12] My parents told me that they had been influenced in calling me "Paul" because of their friendship with him.

there was an immediate response to the appeal. It was a most unusual sight in a morning Bible Reading!"[13]

Maynard had some wonderful support on the committee in spite of the few dissident voices from time to time. Indeed it was good that differing points of view were put. There were many who helped over the years, and I merely mention a few names of those I knew personally. They included Denis Applebee, George Scott, Ron Storey, Gordon Taylor, and Maurice Winterburn. But all, I'm sure, would agree that Maynard, under God, was the mainspring of the Southport International Convention. He loved Holiness Conventions. He had been greatly blessed as a young man at the Battersea Holiness Convention of the I.H.M. and had been Chairman of the inspiring C.H.C. Conventions in the Thirties and Forties. He was now a Church of the Nazarene Minister, but as time went on he was developing a ministry which defied denominational boundaries. He felt at home with all who preached "holiness", and Applebee, Scott, Storey, Taylor and Winterburn were all outside the Church of the Nazarene.[14] We could go on to describe many other meetings of the Convention down the years. I was privileged to be present at a number of them. They had something of the fire of the old Oldham conventions, although perhaps never reaching the same heights. Maynard made a wonderful chairman, always keeping a tight grip on the meetings, and yet radiating joy. Occasionally he might have been a bit domineering, but his sincerity and prayerful spirit more than compensated for this weakness. His prayers at times were most moving and his altar calls turned many a heart closer to the Lord.

During the last three or four years of his life Maynard attended some of the Convention meetings. But he felt rather lost not taking a leading role, and sometimes he would be quite depressed. But by then he was well into his eighties, and he realized in his heart of hearts that he must leave it to others.[15] But it wasn't easy for him. The Convention had been the child of his old age.

---

[13] Flame, November-December 1967, p.31.

[14] The Rev. Denis Applebee was from Emmanuel, Birkenhead, and later with the World Gospel Mission. The Rev. Ron Storey was (and is) with the W.G.M. Mr George Scott worshipped at an independent mission, while Mr Gordon Taylor attended the Brethren Assembly. The Rev. Maurice Winterburn had been an I.H.M. pastor before ordination in the Church of England.

[15] The Convention continues to be held each September, and the present Chairman is the Rev. Ron Storey.

27. _Speakers at the Southport Revival Convention in 1967._
Mentioned in this book are: (l - r)
Seated: centre M.G.J., Dr. Paul Rees. Standing: Major Allister
Smith, 3rd Mr Gordon Taylor, 5th Dr. J. Ford.

28. Elenor Gregory, who became the wife
of C.H.C. leader Clifford Filer.
In late life she married
Rev. Tom Ainscough.

29. Miss Eleanor Howarth -
Flame Secretary. "Without her loving
and loyal service it would have been
impossible for the Flame to have
maintained its worldwide ministry for
four decades." (p.79)

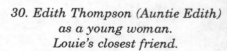

30. Edith Thompson (Auntie Edith)
as a young woman.
Louie's closest friend.

CHAPTER SIXTEEN
THE LATE SIXTIES

The Southport Revival Convention was launched in 1964, and it is to that year that we now return. It was indeed a memorable year for Maynard, for as well as realizing the vision for a convention, it was also the year when he and Louie became settled in their home in Southport - that is if the word "settled" can ever be used to describe Maynard's way of life! Anyway, Southport was to be their home for nearly twenty years.

1964 was also the year of the publication of his most influential book, "*I Believe in the Holy Ghost*". He had been writing this for some time, and several chapters had provided articles for the Flame. But at the end of the year it was published in Britain and could be obtained for four shillings and five pence,[1] including postage from the Flame Secretary. The following year it was re-published in America by the Bethany Fellowship, where it received a much wider circulation. It was later re-published in Britain by Lakeland in conjunction with Bethany Fellowship, and this time reached many of the religious bookshops of the land. I have been unable to find out its exact circulation, although by the early Seventies it had reached 7,000. However, with sales in America and its re-publication in England the total was much greater than this. It was dedicated to me, so I have every reason to remember it!

The book deals with the work of the Holy Spirit in his many outpourings. The opening chapter is called "The Sin of Neglect", and shows how teaching about the Holy Spirit has been ignored. Other chapters cover such subjects as: the Spirit in Creation and in the Bible, the Gifts of the Spirit, the Emblems of the Spirit, and Testimonies to the work of the Spirit. The chapters on the Gifts are very well balanced and won praise from many church leaders, including Dr. Martyn Lloyd-Jones, who wrote: "*I think the way you have handled the question of tongues is quite perfect. I cannot imagine a better statement.*"[2]

Two quotations from the book will give us an impression of its style, range, and biblical basis:

"*We do not read of a single miracle being performed by the sinless Jesus **before** His Jordan baptism. But, on emerging in triumph*

---

[1] 22p. in present currency!

[2] From the quotation on the book cover.

from the wilderness, he went forth to be more than conqueror in every realm into which he entered. Disease vanished at his touch; demons fled before his command; and even the dead came back at his decree. It cannot be over-emphasized that all these miracles were wrought by Jesus in the power of the Holy Spirit who so fully possessed Him. That is why He could make two striking statements: 'I cast out demons by the Spirit of God' (Mt 12:28); and 'he that believeth in me, the works that I do shall he do also; and greater works than these shall he do, because I go unto my Father'".[3]

"The emblem of dew portrays the refreshing and fertilizing power of the Holy Spirit in the soul that is fully yielded to Him. The formation of nature's dew is an object lesson in the rare art of receiving the coveted dew of the Holy Spirit.......Proud and stubborn hearts never sparkle with heavenly dew. It is only the humble and tender-hearted Christian, opening up every avenue of his being to the shining rays of the Sun of righteousness, who glistens with the Graces of the Holy Spirit. Warmed by the indwelling Comforter, he then gives out to others, in thankful service and radiant testimony, of the rich blessings he has received from heaven."[4]

This second quotation points to the strength of the book - its emphasis on the Holy Spirit as the sanctifying agency. The Gifts of the Spirit are treated with great respect and care, and *"tongues"* is regarded as a legitimate gift of the Spirit, provided there are the biblical safeguards. But time and time again Maynard stresses the fact that the Holy Spirit comes to make us holy, as well as empowering for service. (I shall be dealing more fully with the subject of *"tongues"* in a later chapter.)

There was one big sadness in 1964 - the passing of Maynard's close friend Randolph Murray. Maynard was on one of his American visits when news reached him in May that Randolph had died. Maynard wrote:

"We called him the St. Francis of the C.H.C. At our big conventions the saints loved to hear him sing and pray. He had a wonderful gift of lifting a whole audience into the heavenly places as he led us in prayer and pealed out the songs of Zion.

---

[3] I Believe in the Holy Ghost, American edition p.39.

[4] Ibid p.87.

And how he revelled in proclaiming the truth of entire sanctif-
ication which he so beautifully exemplified in his saintly life."[5]

Maynard was now in his sixties and several of his
contemporaries were getting old. When they passed on he felt
their loss keenly, even though he looked forward to the joy of the
resurrection.

The remaining years of the 1960's were packed with campaigns
and conventions, but we shall touch on only a few highlights.

The Flame continued to flourish, and although published by the
Church of the Nazarene, in practice it became an independent
holiness journal. A few years later it became fully independent;
and from May 1971 the magazine was published by the Editors
rather than by the Church of the Nazarene. The Sixties are now
recognized as a time of moral and spiritual decline, but not many
realized it at the time. Maynard, however, blazed away against
the falling standards. For example, he wrote in the Flame in
January 1966:

"The present deplorable state of morals and religion in Britain
invites a search for parallels in our long history. One is surely
found in the 18th century....."[6]

But he wrote with hope, for in the same editorial he went on to
say: *"We go out into the darkness of midnight hour with burning*
lamps. There is much to encourage us. We thank God for the
strenuous efforts being made by godly, enterprising men and
women in preparation for the Billy Graham Crusades in Britain
next June."[7]

In October 1966 Maynard went to the World Congress on
Evangelism held in Berlin. Leading evangelicals from all over
the world attended the conference, including such distinguished
figures as Emperor Hailie Selassie and Dr Billy Graham.
Maynard wrote about his visit in the Flame. He enjoyed the
sweet fellowship he had with many Christians from different
denominations and was touched by the true catholicity of spirit
that existed; he rejoiced at the strong emphasis on the Scriptures;
and he welcomed the stirring challenge to evangelism. On the
other hand, he was sorry that several opportunities for corporate
prayer were missed; he felt that the 18th Century Revival was
not given its proper place; and he very much regretted that there

---

[5] Flame, Summer Number 1964 p.33.

[6] Ibid, p.20.

[7] Ibid, p.21.

was not sufficient emphasis on the sanctifying work of the Holy Spirit. Maynard concluded his article with a call to prayer here in Britain. Could one of the Bible Colleges in Britain be a venue for a Congress of Prayer?[8]

In the years that followed, Maynard valued the Berlin Congress for the contacts it had given him with some outstanding saints. He often talked of Pastor Duma of Durban, South Africa, a simple Baptist Pastor who had been mightily used by God and had even on one occasion been instrumental in raising the dead. Maynard questioned him about this, and became fully convinced that God had indeed used Pastor Duma to perform miracles of New Testament standards.[9]

1967 was another memorable year for Maynard. In it he witnessed both sorrow and joy, his dear friend James Maclagan died in April. Maclagan had been the pioneer of the unity movement in holiness circles, and he was perhaps the leading architect in bringing together the three denominations. Maynard was unable to attend his funeral because he was on tour in the U.S.A. at the time, and in those days America was a long way away! He did, however, put pen to paper for the Flame, which was printed about three weeks after the funeral, and his article was entitled: "*My friend James B. Maclagan*".[10]

In the same year Maynard's closest friend, Jack Ford was awarded a London University Ph.D for his thesis on the Holiness Movements; and which was later published as "*In the Steps of John Wesley*" (a major source for the earlier part of this book). Jack was now the Principal of the Church of the Nazarene College at Didsbury, Manchester; the College having moved to better premises from Glasgow.

One very interesting event in July 1967 was a holiday conference held in the Hotel Rosat at Chateaux d'Oex in Switzerland. It was organized by the Rev. Maurice Winterburn with Maynard as the chief speaker. Louie accompanied him on this busman's holiday "*which both seem to have thoroughly enjoyed*". They met with Christians of several denominations, and in ideal weather saw something of that lovely country; Louie going on a trip to the St. Bernard Pass.

---

[8] Flame, January-February 1967, Editorial.

[9] See also "Take your Glory Lord", Life story of Pastor Duma by Mary Garnett, pp.34 to 37. Published; South African Baptist Missionary Society.

[10] Flame, May - June 1967 p.4.

The following year saw another visit to the States. It would be tedious to go over all the meetings and campaigns, wonderful though many of them were. However, as I have gone through Maynard's diary it is the apparently small things which have caught my eye. The constant references to the reading of the Scriptures, the letters written to loved ones and friends (and Jack Ford is listed several times). Occasionally a really personal note is made in what is otherwise a mere catalogue of happenings. On March 9th 1968, while at Monongahela, Perma, he wrote: *"Finding it difficult to pray. Lord, help me"*.

It must have been about this time that I was approached about becoming Vicar of St.Julian's Church, Shrewsbury. It was a difficult decision to make, but I was conscious of my father's prayers and concern, and he wrote to me several times from America during this period.

Very early in 1969 Maynard received the news that his brother William had died. It was a sad blow. His death was not unexpected as he had been ill for some time, but the sense of loss was nevertheless very real. They had been very close as children, and although they had followed quite different paths, the sense of closeness remained. William, or Willie as Maynard always knew him, had several jobs over the years, but mainly as a driver or salesman for small firms, very rarely travelling outside the South Wales area. He had lived a settled life with his wife Emily and son David, while Maynard, on the other hand, had followed the work of a travelling evangelist with the world as his parish. But at heart they were not far apart, and as we have already mentioned in an early chapter, a photo of Maynard was found in William's wallet when he died.

The funeral took place at Newport, Monmouthshire, on Monday 6th January. Maynard had been preaching at a convention at St. Helens, Lancashire, on Saturday and Sunday, and he and Louie caught a very late train from Liverpool on Sunday night, arriving at Newport in the very early hours of Monday morning, the day of the funeral. The service was at Duckpool Road Baptist Church, as William had remained in the denomination of his upbringing. Maynard has recorded that the service was beautifully conducted by the Rev. Colin Lewis.[11]

Family funerals are both sad and precious. Sad because another one of the family has died but precious because of the renewed links of love and friendship. David, William and Emily's

---

[11] Diary of MGJ. 6th January 1969.

only child, was at this time working in Cardiff as a dentist while at the same time studying for a degree in medicine, and Stephen and I were particularly happy to spend time with our cousin. Emily was shattered by the death of her husband, but welcomed the love and support of her relations; and it was a relief to know that her sister Kitty was close at hand, and would continue to give help in the days ahead. Maynard and Louie did not stay long in Newport, and they arrived back in Southport late that same evening.

The year followed a fairly predictable pattern, with meetings and conventions in various parts of the British Isles. One highlight was a visit in May to the Birmingham Bible Institute where Maynard was a speaker at the annual Open Day. There was a crowd of about 600 in the marquee for the Saturday evening service on 17th May. Although the Institute had some students from Calvinistic backgrounds, this did not inhibit Maynard from preaching from Acts chapter 2: *"When the Day of Pentecost was fully come."* He wrote in his diary that he had great liberty and that there were about twenty seekers. Another highlight that year was the September Revival Convention at Southport, at which David Watson was a main speaker.

At the very end of the year and the decade, Maynard and Louie sailed again for South Africa, for another memorable visit to a country that was constantly in his thoughts and prayers, and for which he was increasingly burdened.

31. South African travellers, Maynard and Louie.

When Maynard and Louie sailed for South Africa in December 1969 they were both old aged pensioners; but Maynard was to have another fifteen years of full-time ministry before age, bereavement, and sickness finally made him retire. The visit to Africa was typical of many of his remaining tours and campaigns. It was packed with meetings in many different areas. There was never any difficulty in getting invitations.

As we shall see in a later chapter, Maynard was forming definite views about Africa, and he did not feel that the full integration of the races was either desirable or biblical.[1] The early part of the tour was spent in the Cape Province and Maynard and Louie stayed with Captain and Mrs Dobbie; and when they left South Africa six months later, their last visit was to the home of the Dobbies. Maynard wrote in his diary: "*Very sacred time at the home of the Captain. Departed with mixed feelings. Shall we see them again on earth? He (the Lord) knows.*"[2] I don't think they did meet again as Captain and Mrs Dobbie both died before his next African visit. Captain G.S. Dobbie was very well known in evangelical circles in South Africa, having been the Principal of Glenvar Bible College, and also interested in many holiness projects. The Dobbie Family was also very well known in the British Army; the most famous member being the war hero, General Dobbie of Malta. Captain Dobbie himself was a holder of the Military Cross.

Part of the tour was spent in Rhodesia, where there was much blessing in many of the meetings. It was during this visit that Maynard was granted an interview with the Prime Minister, Mr Ian Smith. Maynard had prayed for him for several years, and admired his stand of Unilateral Independence for Rhodesia. Maynard met Ian Smith on June 18th 1970, and he assured him of his prayers. In typical Maynard fashion he asked Mr Smith if he would like a prayer, and the Prime Minister solemnly bowed his head while Maynard prayed.[3]

Maynard and Louie returned to England via Athens and Israel, and they were able to spend about six days in the Holy Land,

---

[1] Flame, May-June 1970, and see chapter 18, final section, p.29,30.

[2] Diary 30th July 1970.

[3] Flame, September-October 1970 and diary, p.32.

which they much enjoyed, visiting many of the places where our Lord had ministered.

They returned home to Southport on the 12th August. Most men would have taken a week or two's holiday, but Maynard left Southport two days later for meetings in Wrexham and Llay, North Wales!

Louie was very much at home in Southport, and by the early Seventies had made many friends. It was also very much a family home, although we were all grown up with families of our own. Kenneth had been working in Canada, where his daughter Gillian was born. In 1971 he moved to Rhodesia with his wife and baby daughter, and in Salisbury David was added to the family. But they were in Rhodesia for only a short time, for in 1973 they moved to Johannesburg, where Kenneth established an insurance business. They visited the United Kingdom from time to time, and always spent several days at Arundel Road. Stephen was an airline pilot with Laker Airways, and lived in Horsham with his wife Marjorie and their three daughters, Sara, Louise and Rachel. He too often called at Southport. I was Vicar of St. Julian's, Shrewsbury, from 1968 to 1976, and from 1976 onwards Vicar of Holy Trinity, Shrewsbury. Southport was only 90 miles away, so I was a frequent visitor. Indeed, it did not seem like a visit - it was always home from home, at least while Louie was alive. I loved going over to see "Mum and Dad" and was always given a royal welcome. Very occasionally Stephen, Kenneth and I would manage to be together at the same time.

As Maynard grew older he did spend a little more time at home, especially as the Southport Convention took such a great deal of preparation. But nearly all the home chores were left to Louie.

It was a happy home, with lots of visitors. One very frequent guest was Gordon Taylor. He was the son of the late Pastor James Taylor who had been a speaker at the Oldham Conventions and lecturer at Beech Lawn College. Gordon worshipped at the Brethren Assembly at Southport, but was a firm believer in the teaching of the holiness Movements. Gordon became almost another son to Louie, and a few years later she made request that he preach at her funeral. He married Dorothy in April 1969, but even after establishing a home of his own he kept in close touch with Maynard and Louie. He was for many years one of the main organizers of the Southport Convention.

Louie was a very warm person, and had several close friends. She still kept in touch with Miss Thompson (Auntie Edith) from Ashton, but also built up friendships with folk at Southport. Her best friend in Southport was Doris Scott, who, along with her husband George, worshipped at Boundary Street Mission. They became like sisters, and it was a terrible blow when Doris died at the age of seventy-five, in 1977. Even after this bereavement, Louie maintained close links with the Scott family, and especially with Betty, Doris's daughter-in-law. Another good friend was Mrs Connie Winter, who worshipped at the Elim Church. She was a very practical and straightforward person, who became particularly close when Louie developed cancer a few years later, taking over many of the day to day responsibilities which were becoming too much for a very sick person. Ron and Margaret Storey from the World Gospel Mission were also good friends of both Louie and Maynard, as were Jim and Nora Pilling from the Methodist Church.

Thus they made many friends with folk from different evangelical Churches in Southport. Maynard would worship in one or other of the Southport churches on his occasional free Sundays. He felt very much at home in Christ Church (Anglican) on Lord Street. They used an easy-to-follow service and this gave him confidence in dealing with the Prayer Book! He found the clergy of that Church to be fine men of God, who gave sound, biblical sermons. I went with him one evening to a mid-week Bible study when Geoffrey Hart was the Vicar. A large number of people gathered for a scholarly exposition of Scripture.[4]

Maynard loved the golf links in Southport. He would walk for miles on the Royal Birkdale or the Hillside courses, and much of this time was spent in prayer.

In all, the Seventies were very happy years for both of them, although there was the increasing sadness of departed friends; and the next few years were to see the deaths of Maynard's two closest friends - Clifford Filer and Jack Ford. (The other member of the Four, Leonard Ravenhill, is still alive at the time of writing, and continues to live in the United States. Maynard was in touch with him right up to his own death.)

Clifford was the first to go. He had a very severe heart attack while working as Pastor at Llay, North Wales. However, he seemed to make a good recovery and took up his work again. But shortly afterwards he had another severe attack and died on 15th January, 1971.

Maynard led the funeral service at the Llay Nazarene Church, which was packed to capacity. The platform was crowded with

---

[4] The Rev. Geoffrey Hart later became Rector of Cheltenham.

about thirty Ministers; and I was privileged to be one of them. The singing was electrifying, and I particularly remember "*I will sing the wondrous story*" and "*And I know that my Redeemer lives*" (to the tune "*Torquay*"). Jack Ford gave a moving tribute, and Albert Lown touched the spiritual heights in his prayer. Maynard himself gave the main address, in which he described Clifford as "*a Prince in Israel*". He had outstanding pastoral gifts, and was a man of prayer: "*He lived daily in intimate communion with the Lord whom he so dearly loved.*" Maynard looked back on their forty years together, and especially to the early pioneer days of the Calvary Holiness Church. Clifford and his wife Elenor had been missionaries in Colombia during difficult days, and they had made great sacrifices to bring the Gospel to some of the people of a dark and needy country. Maynard remembered the family. He had known Elenor since the Manchester Tabernacle days, and in more recent days he had frequently stayed in their home in England, so he knew their grown up children very well - Paulina, Esther, and Philip.[5]

The Committal was at the Wrexham Crematorium. I remember it well, because I gave a lift to another C.H.C. veteran - Harold Hawkins.

It was nearly ten years later that Jack Ford died, in September 1980. He had retired as Principal of the Nazarene College in 1973, and spent several profitable years in lighter pastoral duties, mainly at Heysham. He became ill in the summer of 1980 and was taken to Airedale Hospital, Steeton, Keighley.

Maynard visited him the day before he died. He has written of that last encounter:

"*He was still the same gracious, patient man of God I had known for many years. Then I did something I have never done before. I gently kissed his forehead and told him he was precious to me. Almost in a whisper, but audibly, he replied: 'And you are precious to me.' Then with characteristic thoughtfulness, he referred to our three sons, Paul, Stephen and Kenneth. He knew them well; and they had always highly esteemed their father's life-long friend, Dr. Ford. Mustering the remnants of his fast ebbing strength, he told me slowly of his concern for our Zion - the Church of the Nazarene. In essence he whispered: 'She is going through a time of crisis, but there are signs of encouragement'. I*

---

[5] Flame, February-March 1971 p.27.

wished him goodbye for the last time.... Next day Brother Ford had gone from the scene of time."[6]

The funeral took place on 29th September 1980, at Keighley Parish Church, the building being loaned to the Church of the Nazarene for the occasion. The Rev. T.W. Schofield, Superintendent Minister of the Church of the Nazarene, led the service, with several tributes from pastors and friends. Maynard gave the main address (which took twenty-five minutes). He made his own tribute to Jack - his best friend for over fifty years. They first met at the Trekkers' campaign in Hull, and ever since they had toiled together in the work of holiness. He was a most gracious man, a fine pastor, and an able scholar. But where has he gone? Maynard then went on to give a challenge to be ready for our own home-calling, concluding with the lines of the well-known hymn: *"I hear Thy welcome voice, that calls me now to Thee."*

Maynard recorded in his diary that he *"felt the help of the precious Holy Spirit."* It was indeed a traumatic time for Maynard. I don't think he ever expected to outlive his younger friend. Although they were so different, Maynard always knew he could depend on Jack. They could be very forthright with one another and not lose love. Now only two of the original four remained - himself and Leonard Ravenhill.

Dr Jack Ford's contribution to the Holiness movement in Britain is immense and has never been fully appreciated. Not only did he help to found the Calvary Holiness Church, but he was also its best thinker and scholar. When the C.H.C. was merged with the Church of Nazarene his scholarship was well used. He was very much at home in the Church of the Nazarene and settled down to it much more than Maynard. Although he believed in the gifts of the Holy Spirit, I think that for practical purposes he felt sufficient freedom in the larger denomination. He also appreciated the better facilities and the worldwide fellowship.

During this period Maynard lost many other friends on earth. Even before Clifford's death Sister Lucy Taylor had passed to glory (October 1969), and between the deaths of Clifford and Jack there were to be many others. William Williams of Bargoed, who had so greatly influenced Maynard as a young man died on 31st July 1971. Maynard conducted the funeral service. He wrote in his diary of *"a melting peace"*. Pastor Harry Toft, died in 1972,

---

[6] Flame, November-December 1980 p.17, 18.

as did Dr George Frame. The following year saw the passing of Captain Dobbie, and 1974 the death of Dr Jessop in the United States. Three years later Dr Arthur Fawcett joined the departed heroes, and in 1978 Major Allister Smith died shortly after being involved in a car crash in South Africa.

Major Smith was one of Maynard's closest friends during the Sixties and Seventies. They were both valiant prophets of holiness, and never afraid to speak their minds. The Major was in full flight until the end, with articles in the Flame and full preaching engagements.

Louie also lost close friends during this period. We have already referred to Mrs Scott. But Louie's much older friend, Edith Thompson, died in December 1979 at the age of ninety one. In spite of several severe illnesses over the years, she enjoyed reasonable health, and serious deafness was her main handicap. She was thrilled to reach the age of ninety and we had a little party in her home in Ashton-u-Lyne. Somehow her ninety-first birthday passed with little notice, and then just a few months later she was found dead at the bottom of her stairs. She had no telephone, and although friends usually kept in constant touch with her, she was not found until a day or two after her death. We all felt very guilty and sad, and hoped that she had passed away without any pain. She had been an outstanding friend to the family and to many other families.

Her funeral took place on the 21st December in her beloved Ashton where she had lived for so many years, and where she had had her shop. The service was taken by her Pastor, the Rev. Leonard McNeil, and I read the lesson from 1 Corinthians 15 and Maynard gave a short address. There were not many people present at the Ashton Mission. She had outlived her friends, and I don't think the regular congregation at the Mission realized what a spiritual giant she had been. She could be rather crusty and very blunt, and her hearing became very poor in old age, so she had not been able to forge links with the younger generation. But it was good to see Eva Caldwell (née Steele), along with her daughter Pauline. Edith had been practically a mother to Eva in earlier years. There were also a few others at the funeral who had come to know Auntie Edith, including Mrs Alice Sykes from Ashton who had become very close and was extremely upset by her death. Maynard wrote in his diary:

"Funeral in Ashton Church of the Nazarene at 10.30 a.m. Very few present. Service conducted by Bro. McNeil. Paul read Scriptures and gave a brief and beautiful tribute to "Auntie"

*Edith.   Cremation   at   Dukinfield   Crematorium.   Poignant
memories!*" (The underlining is Maynard's.)

In early August 1974 Maynard was troubled by his prostate
gland.   On the night of Monday 4th August he was in
considerable pain, but insisted on preaching the next morning.
However, he had to give in and was taken to Southport
Infirmary. His diary records that he continued to work from his
bed, both writing and telephoning. On the following Monday he
went down to theatre for the operation. He still managed to
write in his diary that evening:

*"Wonderful sense of God's dear presence - His peace in my heart.
Down in theatre about 1½ hours. Dear Louie came to see me in
the evening."*

He stayed in hospital until the 24th August, when he wrote in
his diary: *"Hallelujah! A million thanks to Jesus and my deep
gratitude to the many saints who have prayed for me during this
testing time."*   In 1974 a prostate gland operation was more
serious than it is today, and this was one of the very few times
that Maynard had experienced real physical discomfort. It was
perhaps a preparation for the far greater testing that was to
come.

The mid-Seventies saw the retirement of Miss Eleanor Howarth
as Flame Secretary, due to age and ill health. We have already
paid tribute to her outstanding contribution to the work of the
Flame, extended over thirty years. Maynard was blessed in his
Flame Secretaries, for although Miss Howarth served far longer
than anyone else and gave herself to the task as no-one else
could, she was followed by another able Secretary, the Rev.
Arthur Sowerbutts, who took over in the autumn of 1975 and
continued until after Maynard himself retired.

But the Seventies did not consist only of bereavements,
setbacks, and retirements. Maynard even at this late phase of
life was making new friendships. The Rev. Denis Applebee from
Emmanuel, Birkenhead, became a constant visitor to 35 Arundel
Road, and he and Maynard became like brothers. He also struck
up a very happy partnership with a much younger man - Alec
Passmore. Alec had been trained at Cliff College, and was a keen
trekker.   During the Seventies he and Maynard held several
campaigns together, and Maynard very much enjoyed the
fellowship of the younger man. Mrs Mair Perkins, the beautiful
soprano singer from Cardiff, became a close friend of both Louie
and Maynard, and during her illness in 1977 Maynard prayed for
her, and she received a very real touch from the Lord.

Maynard made many interesting journeys, including another visit to Southern Africa in 1976, when Louie again went with him. They arrived in Johannesburg in April, and were met by Kenneth and Hazel, and Maynard's grandson David. Most of May and early June was spent in Rhodesia, for which Maynard had a great burden. He wrote in the Flame of the meetings of great blessing, with very real repentance being evident. Rhodesia was going through difficult days. Sanctions were beginning to bite and the guerilla war was taking its toll. Worst of all was the outside pressure to abdicate to African nationalism. In mid-June they travelled to Capetown where they stayed with Peggy Dobbie, the daughter of the late Captain and Mrs G.S. Dobbie, and a fine, Spirit-filled woman. Her black maid Hannah was also a delightful Christian, and it was one of the joys of being in that home to share morning prayers with Peggy and Hanna. While at Diep River, Capetown, Maynard preached at the Docks Mission, with a congregation of five hundred.

They returned to Johannesburg in mid-July, where Maynard took part in a Crusade at the Central Baptist Church, before returning to the U.K. on the 20th July.

The late Seventies were still a very busy time for Maynard, in spite of his age. During 1977 he was engaged in meetings throughout the country, which included a visit to the Bible College of Wales, Swansea, where he was a special speaker.

One very happy feature of this period was Maynard's renewal of links with Cliff College. The Rev. Dr Arthur Skevington Wood was Principal and they had known one another for a number of years. Dr Wood had written articles in the Flame and had a close association with the Holiness movement. He has written warmly of his friendship with Maynard; [7] and he has described Maynard as one who *"embodied all that Cliff has stood for since its inception"*. Whenever Maynard appeared at the Spring Bank Holiday Anniversary Services he would be asked to pray at one of the meetings. In 1978 he was invited to be one of the speakers. The Cliff Anniversary is a splendid affair, which draws thousands from all over the country, and at which there are very eminent speakers. Maynard felt honoured to be among them, but he was even more pleased that "holiness" was being taught at the College in a way that would have warmed the heart of the late Samuel Chadwick.

---

[7] Preface to "Third Wave and Second Coming", published 1992 by the Flame Trust.

Later that summer he set out for a visit to Hungary with Mr Edward Marshall. Mr Marshall paid numerous visits behind the Iron Curtain, and he asked Maynard to accompany him on this trip. It was not altogether a success as the car had problems and they did not reach Hungary. However, they had some interesting visits to parts of the Continent, including one night at Darmstadt at the remarkable "Canaan Settlement" of the Sisters of Mary, who had built the settlement amongst the bombed ruins of the city as a direct answer to prayer at the conclusion of the Second World War.

The following year included another visit to South Africa, which would be his last preaching visit to that country. Louie and Maynard flew from Heathrow on April 20th, 1979. I remember it well, because my car received a knock while parked at the airport! Again they stayed with Kenneth and Hazel, before commencing his preaching tour. But let Maynard speak for himself:

"*After ten weeks of extensive travel in the Transvaal, Natal, and the Cape we are now on the last lap before returning home on 20th July. It has been a joy to preach in Wesleyan, Nazarene, Baptist and Lutheran churches, and to students in two Bible colleges (black and white). In addition has been the sweetness of renewed fellowship with many friends and colleagues of yester-year. it has pleased the Lord to let us see hundreds of earnest seekers in various campaigns in the past weeks. We look forward to Him for a glorious climax on our final Sunday when we preach at two rallies in Soweto.*"[8]

Writing later of those Soweto meetings, he records that there were 700 Zulus who gathered to "*sing, pray, testify, and hear the Word of God.*" [9] It was indeed a fitting climax to his wonderful visits to South Africa, where his ministry had been mightily blessed. He would visit South Africa just once again, but under entirely different circumstances. The delightful highlight of the following year was the Golden Wedding of Maynard and Louie. They had been married in Bargoed on 2nd April 1930, and fifty years later they celebrated their half-century by a visit to the Holy Land and by a family gathering in Southport.

Sir Freddie Laker was still in full swing with his Laker Airways, and Stephen was one of his most senior pilots. As a token of his appreciation of Stephen's work for the company Sir

---

[8] Flame, September-October 1979, p.32.

[9] Ibid p.35.

Freddie gave free return tickets to Maynard and Louie to Israel. They flew to Tel Aviv on 18th March 1980, and almost immediately upon landing had fellowship with other evangelical Christians. They visited several of the holy sites, including the Wailing Wall, the Sea of Tiberias, Jacob's Well, Nazareth and Capernaum. They rejoiced to stand where the blessed Lord had stood, and they worshipped on Sunday morning, 23rd March, at the Garden Tomb, where they experienced "*An unforgettable Service*".[10] Maynard was never one to be off duty for long, and that evening he preached at the Nazarene Church in Jerusalem. They returned to England at the end of the month.

Later that year, on 14th July, there was a family dinner at the Scarisbrick Hotel, Southport. Kenneth and Hazel were over from South Africa, and there was a wonderful Golden Wedding meal. Father, mother, and the three sons with some of their families came together to share love and thanksgiving. Maynard wrote in his diary: "*Had a memorable evening. Real gratitude to God for his goodness and mercy.*" He was now seventy eight years of age and Louie seventy five. Neither of them seemed old. Maynard was still travelling the world, and Louie, in spite of aches and pains, seemed to be enjoying good health. It was perhaps the highlight of their old age.

32. Louie with grandchildren, Gillian & David (children of Kenneth & Hazel).

---

[10] Diary, 23rd March 1980.

CHAPTER EIGHTEEN

CONSTANT CONTROVERSY

This is perhaps a good point to examine some of the issues which Maynard faced during his long Ministry.

Holiness Teaching

His main battle was always to maintain the teaching of Scriptural holiness as he understood it. Of course, all true believers teach that holiness is important, and this is one of the main themes of the Keswick Convention. But where "the holiness folk" (of whom Maynard was one) differed was that they believed with Wesley that sin could be dealt with at source. The Rev. David Lambert (father of Principal Lambert) wrote a masterly letter to Maynard on this subject which was printed in the Flame several years later. [1]

*"**Holiness People** are those who believe that it is the New Testament teaching that by committal to Jesus Christ the human nature can be purified from the disposition to sin.......Reader Harris was right in his challenge to "Keswick" that there is no one verse of Scripture saying that the sinful disposition we are all born with must remain until death.....* (But David Lambert goes on to show that there is a human factor in holiness experience.) *I am more than ever sure that Oswald Chambers' insight is of great value and is true - that our sin-cleansed human nature remains, but not as a sinful thing. It is morally neutral, yet it is not saintly, it needs bridging by daily intelligent decision under the transfiguring power of the Holy Spirit so that sainthood grows by a steady process."*

Maynard himself had experienced this heart-cleansing as a *"Second Blessing"* when he was a young man (see chapter two), and he continued to emphasize it throughout his ministry. He preached countless sermons on this experience, and there were frequent articles in the Flame. There is no need to go over the whole story, because the fight for this teaching has been perhaps the main theme of this book.

But there can be little doubt that this emphasis was the cause of many doors being closed. Many discerning people, for example, the Rev. Herbert McGonigle, have publicly stated that they regarded Maynard as one of the outstanding preachers of his day. Yet he was rarely asked to preach at the great evangelical rallies

---

[1] Flame, March-April 1963, p.27.

and he was never invited to speak at the Keswick Convention. It is only fair to add that a few - very few - speakers holding Maynard's views on Sanctification were invited to speak at the Keswick convention, and these included Maynard's close friends Dr Paul Rees and Major Allister Smith. Maynard was thrilled that they were asked and never - to my knowledge - showed any disappointment that he himself was not included. Yet although many doors were closed to him, plenty of others were opened, including Anglican, Pentecostal, and Baptist pulpits. He also had a good relationship with a few like-minded Methodist leaders, such as Dr. Arthur Skevington Wood and Dr. W.R. Davies; but he was only occasionally asked to preach in Methodist chapels - somewhat surprising when it is remembered that Maynard's theology was thoroughly Wesleyan, and that he was trained at a Methodist College.[2]

There can be no doubt that Maynard played a vital role in helping to maintain "*holiness*" teaching in Britain during the Twentieth Century. It is difficult to assess the number of churches in Britain that have kept this emphasis because of Maynard. There were twenty-seven C.H.C. congregations when that movement became part of the Church of the Nazarene, and Maynard's influence on the present day Church of the Nazarene in Britain has been a lasting one. As Dr. Lown has written: "*A good percentage of mature Nazarene members (in Britain) entered into 'heart holiness' under his ministry.*"[3] But his influence was far wider than this, for the Flame was read by numerous Christians from varying denominations, and his books and sermons, and travels in several parts of the world have encouraged thousands to believe that God could deal with their sinful self. He has also had an effect on the Charismatic and Pentecostal movements in this country, as we shall see in the next section.

The Gifts of the Spirit - particularly the gift of tongues.

Another battle was over the gifts of the Spirit. He never spoke in tongues himself, but he felt nevertheless that this could be a gift of the Holy Spirit.

---

[2] There were, of course, many friendships with Methodists over the years, and in earlier days these included the Rev. Percy Hassam and Pastor James Taylor. However, they were never as numerous as might be expected.

[3] Letter to author, 16th March 1992.

As a young man he had a salutary experience with regard to the gift of tongues, and this experience never left him. It is best told in Maynard's own words:

"*As a young Christian I was for years prejudiced against the 'Pentecostal' Movement. Their special emphasis on speaking in other tongues as the indispensable evidence of the Baptism of Spirit was contrary to my own 'Pentecost'...... Unfortunately my prejudice against the 'Tongues' people reached the point when, from the pulpit, I openly denounced speaking in other tongues as being of Satan.*

I was yet to learn that there are three sources of 'other tongues' - divine, demonic, and psychic. The revelation of this important truth came not through any talented preacher, but through the victorious, prayerful life of a servant girl named Grace Langston. This humble and radiant young lady was a member of a small holiness group who worshipped in Cathays Terrace, Cardiff. In all the years I had known her she had never spoken with other tongues in public services. Grace was one of the most reliable and consistent witnesses to scriptural Holiness I had ever met.

During a heated argument one evening with a somewhat dogmatic Pentecostalist I was amazed to hear him retort, 'But Grace Langston speaks in tongues'. Of course I did not believe him. Instead I met Grace herself and asked the question.

'Do you speak in tongues, Grace?'

To my astonishment, she replied quietly, 'Yes, praise God, I do.'"[4]

Maynard recorded that he never again condemned the Pentecostals for speaking in tongues, and he was to have sweet fellowship with many of them until the end of his life.

We have already seen in an earlier chapter (chapter five) how Maynard made a stand on this issue with the I.H.M. hierarchy and it was one of the reasons why he and the other Three left that denomination in 1934.

We have also seen the argument that arose when the C.H.C. merged with the Church of the Nazarene (see chapter twelve). But for several years after the merger it seemed an academic issue. Maynard continued to write articles on the subject, and these appeared from time to time in the Flame, but as very few in the holiness congregations spoke in tongues it was hardly a matter of division.

---

[4] Flame, March-April 1985 p.10.

But then came the Charismatic Movement of the Sixties, when Christians all over the world began to discover the gifts of the Spirit as outlined in 1 Corinthians 12. In the United States an Episcopal Rector, the Rev. Dennis Bennett wrote a startling book, entitled "Nine o'clock in the Morning", in which he told the story of his own Pentecostal experience and the renewal of his congregation. In England, Michael Harper, a curate of All Souls, Langham Place, the Mecca of Evangelical Christianity in the Church of England, spoke in other tongues and encouraged others to do the same. At the Keswick Convention of 1965, several of the leaders were alarmed and spoke against the movement. My father and I were together at that Convention, and he became very stirred up. This was no longer an academic question. Mighty men and women of God were claiming supernatural gifts, and as in the I.H.M. days other leaders were denying their scriptural experience.

Maynard returned from Keswick convinced that the Holy Spirit was at work, and although the movement had to be tested he was becoming more and more certain that men like Michael Harper should be encouraged. The Flame contained articles on the charismatic movement, and some of its outstanding leaders were invited to the Southport Convention. In his book "I Believe in the Holy Ghost", which was written early in this revival, Maynard again upheld the importance of the gifts of the Holy Spirit, while always subordinating them to the fruit of the Spirit. But he continued to stress that *tongues* was not for everyone. In the mid-Sixties charismatic leaders were tending to say that *tongues* was the evidence of the Baptism of the Holy Spirit. Maynard refuted this error in his book, as he had done in preaching and articles for many years. His position was clear. The Gifts are to be distributed as the Spirit wills. The Fruit, on the other hand, is to be demonstrated by all sanctified Christians. Whereas the Gifts represent the power of Christ, the Fruit is the character of Jesus which all are called to portray. Indeed it is only *"the truly sanctified, Spirit-filled Christians who know how to exercise in meekness the gifts of the Holy Spirit."* [5]

It would have been hoped that all holiness people would go along with such a balanced view, which Dr. Martyn Lloyd-Jones called *"quite perfect"*. Such, however, was not the case. Maynard was opposed on numerous occasions, but always stuck to his position. As editor of the Flame he continued to publish articles

---

[5] "I Believe in the Holy Ghost", American edition, p. 120.

in sympathy with the charismatic movement, although always cautious of its excesses.

It was in the Seventies, however, that the controversy really flared up. Although Maynard was himself over seventy years of age, he was in good health and still travelling the world. In June 1976 the General Assembly of the Church of the Nazarene met in Dallas, Texas. The President, the Rev. Dr. Eugene Stowe gave the Quadrennial address. Maynard was not present, but he read the report later in the summer when he returned from South Africa.[6] He was shocked. One paragraph read:

"The Board of Superintendents is unanimous in its agreement that 'it is our considered judgement and ruling that any practice and/or propagation of speaking in tongues either as evidence of the Baptism with the Holy Spirit or as a neo-Pentecostal ecstatic prayer language shall be interpreted as inveighing against the doctrines and usages of the Church of the Nazarene.'"

Maynard wrote to Dr Stowe, protesting about this statement: *"It is with genuine sorrow and heaviness of heart that I would draw your attention to a small section of your quadrennial Address..... I agree that the propagation of speaking in tongues **as the evidence** of the Baptism of the Holy Spirit does inveigh against the doctrines of the Church of the Nazarene. But for the Board of General Superintendents to publicly declare that it is 'their considered judgement and ruling that any practice of speaking in tongues as a neo-Pentecostal prayer language shall be inveighing against the Church of the Nazarene' is, in my judgement, **Unscriptural, Divisive, and A Serious Breach of Contract**."*

Maynard gave his reasons, quoting 1 Corinthians 12 and 14, and stressing the fact that many saintly Christians speak in tongues, including some members of the Church of Nazarene. He also reminded the General Superintendent of the contract made in January 1955 when the C.H.C. was merged with the Church of the Nazarene.

In the letter Maynard summed up his own position regarding *"tongues"* as: *"Seek not; forbid not"*. He concluded by stating that he was writing partly out of duty to those former 27 C.H.C. Churches who had joined the Church of the Nazarene.

Maynard sent copies of his letter to several friends, including Dr Jack Ford, Mr Norman Grubb, Dr Paul Rees, and the Rev. David Tarrant.

---

[6] Diary 23rd August 1976.

Dr Stowe replied on 11th September 1976. He denied that his Statement was anti-Scriptural and referred to an article to be printed in the Herald of Holiness (see below). He went on to say that the statement was far from divisive and had the overwhelming support of 35,000 people at the Assembly. Finally, He denied that there was any form of contract with the old C.H.C.

Maynard wrote again on 24th September, in which he restated his position, but left aside for the moment the contract that had been made in 1955. He was, however, at the same time in touch with Jack Ford to try to establish the legal position.

On 15th October, the Herald of Holiness was published, with the article mentioned by Dr. Stowe. It included the following paragraph:

"Early in its history the Church of the Nazarene stated its opposition to tongues-speaking as taught and practised by the so-called Pentecostal groups......... the gift of tongues is related to the miraculous gift of many languages on the day of Pentecost.......
We believe that the biblical material supports one authentic gift - a language given to communicate the gospel and not an unknown babble of sounds. It is our understanding that in 1 Corinthians 12: 13, 14 Paul was seeking to prevent the abuse of the authentic gift and was condemning that which was spurious and of the flesh. We believe that the religious exercise called 'tongues' which is not a means of communicating truth is a false gift and a dangerous substitute. We do not believe in a so-called prayer language."

This was more than an ordinary article for it was signed by six General Superintendents. It was the official view of the leaders of the Church of the Nazarene.

In early November Maynard received a telephone call from Mary Allison, a reporter from the Kansas City Star; and shortly afterwards an article appeared on the front page of the Newspaper, entitled: *"Speaking in tongues sharply divides Church of Nazarene"*. The article made an assessment of the controversy, and quoted Maynard himself:

"Perhaps the person most upset over the issue is the Rev. Maynard G. James who was President of the Calvary Holiness Church (C.H.C.) in the British Isles when that church merged with the Church of the Nazarene in 1955. In a telephone interview from his home in England, Mr James said that his Church 'would never have joined the Church of the Nazarene without the assurance that its followers could follow their own

conscience in the matter of tongues. We have happy fellowship with godly pentecostal (charismatic) people. There is no issue here. As far as we in Britain are concerned there is no need to bring it up'. The C.H.C. had broken off from its former denomination largely because that denomination forbade speaking in tongues. 'We did not advocate speaking in tongues in the C.H.C.,' Mr James said, 'But we did not forbid it. It (our stand) was in keeping with 1 Corinthians 12 to 14'. (First Corinthians 14: 39 says: 'Forbid not to speak in tongues'.)

"Dr Eugene Stowe, spokesman for the Board of General Superintendents, said in a telephone interview that there had never been any evidence - only hearsay - that the merger of the Church of the Nazarene Church and the British Church included an agreement to allow tongue speaking....... Mr James, however, said: 'It may be they did not record it in Kansas City; that is their own affair. But we have it definitely in black and white.'" [7]

On 26th November Dr Stowe wrote again to Maynard. He was obviously disturbed by the article in the Kansas City Star Newspaper. He claimed the reporter was really from a charismatic magazine, and he accused her of trying to cause division. Regarding the "understanding" of 1955, he referred Maynard to Dr Charles Strickland, though he himself did not believe any undertaking had been made about tongues speaking.

It is not clear whether Maynard did correspond with Dr Strickland, but he did receive two important letters from Dr Ford on the subject. On 5th October 1976, Dr Ford wrote:

"The fact that there is no record of the agreement reached at the meeting between the Nazarene Advisory Board of the C.H.C Executive Council on February 8th and 9th 1955 does not invalidate the 'The Basis of Agreement'. This was accepted by the Nazarene Advisory Board who were empowered to act on behalf of the General Church."

In a later letter dated 11th December 1976, Dr Ford added that the Minutes of the meeting of 12th April 1955, of the Delegates Conference Meeting clearly showed that the Joint meeting of the C.H.C. Executive Council and Church of the Nazarene Advisory Council were given power to effect the Union.

It may be that the actual proof of a fully legal undertaking is in dispute, but that an understanding was reached is clear from the evidence produced by Dr Ford, and fully documented in his book, "In the Steps of John Wesley" which was accepted as a doctorate

---

[7] Kansas City Star, 13th November 1976.

thesis at London University.[8] It was published by the Church of the Nazarene itself long before this contention arose. Maynard would never have joined the Church of Nazarene unless he had been assured on the freedom of the gifts of the Spirit. He had not forgotten the issue of 1934.

Maynard felt betrayed. He thought he had been dealing with brothers in the Lord and not clever lawyers who would turn the situation around. It is to his great credit that he did not become bitter. As he had said in the telephone conversation with the Kansas City Reporter, it was not a real issue in the British Churches, and he continued to have close fellowship with the holiness folk in Britain. But he never went to the United States again. And although a Nazarene minister until his dying day, he felt the ties with Headquarters had been broken - and not by him!

However, his ministry continued unabated, and he was still welcome at many Nazarene pulpits all over the world. But at a deep level there was a serious breach which would not be healed in his life time.

For a few more years Maynard continued as editor of the Flame, and in it he fiercely maintained his position. For example, in November 1976, he wrote:

"Injunctions to forbid any form of tongues-speaking and praying, whether in private or public are bound to grieve the Holy Spirit."[9]

Maynard received a number of encouraging letters at this time, including ones from Norman Grubb, Barry Walton, Frank Mitchell, John Crouch, and Peggy Dobbie (South Africa). The only one which gave any support to the contrary position was from David Tarrant, a Church of the Nazarene District Superintendent Minister from Glasgow.

For the rest of his life Maynard was to receive letters on this subject. Some of them were from Nazarene ministers in the United States who were in real distress. Out of revival in their churches had come a prayer gift of speaking in tongues. They found themselves in an impossible position. I even received letters and phone calls myself, especially when Maynard was very old and ill. One of the most important letters that Maynard received was from Dr J. Wesley Adams, who in March 1983 sent Maynard a copy of his resignation letter. He had been Associate Professor of Biblical Studies at a Nazarene Seminary, the Mid-American Nazarene College. He opposed the 1976 statements

---

[8] See S.J.W., especially pages 169 - 174.

[9] Flame, November-December 1976, p.23.

and had been asked to resign. He did so by way of an open letter in which he deplored the attitude of the Church of the Nazarene on the issue of speaking in tongues. A year later Maynard received a desperate letter from Pastor Dan Brady, who had been a Church of the Nazarene minister in Ohio, and had lost his pastorate because of his stand on *tongues*.

At the time of writing the matter is still not resolved. Maynard was to carry this sadness with him to the grave. But his stand for what he regarded as biblical truth was all the more remarkable when it is realized that he himself never spoke in tongues, nor ever regarded it as a major gift. The fact that it was a gift that God himself could bestow was enough for him.

But his stand has a further significance. It kept the door open between the holiness groups and pentecostal groups in Britain. Maynard is remembered with honour and affection in many pentecostal and charismatic churches, and his emphasis on both the fruit and gifts of the Spirit was appreciated by many. In the parish in which I worked in Shrewsbury, the local Apostolic Church pastor, the Rev. Omri Bowen, told me how much he had been encouraged by Maynard's ministry.

As we have seen in previous chapters, Maynard had close links with several charismatic and pentecostal leaders, including David Watson, Michael Harper, David Pawson, Arthur Wallis, and Alex Tee (Elim). They all emphasised Christian holiness as the important result of the Baptism of the Holy Spirit, even though they may not have used Maynard's phraseology.

In the United States Norman Grubb and Leonard Ravenhill, amongst others, have maintained this twin emphasis, although the Church of the Nazarene seems to have slammed the door against charismatic insights and experience. Maynard was desperately disappointed at the outcome of his protest; but his battle for truth can never really be lost, as the Holy Spirit is the Spirit of truth.

The Israel Identity and kindred subjects.

The question of Israel's identity was never as big a controversy as the tongues issue. Nevertheless it played an important part in Maynard's thinking and writing. But first let me define what is meant by "The Israel Identity".

Under King Solomon the Children of Israel had been one nation, although consisting of twelve tribes. After his death, however, the Kingdom was divided into two: the House of Israel to the North and the House of Judah to the South. Israel has never been one nation from that day to this.

Both Houses disobeyed God, and He warned them that they would be severely punished and taken into captivity. These prophecies were fulfilled to the letter. In 722 B.C. Samaria was captured by the Assyrians and this meant the end of the Northern Kingdom. The House of Judah survived for well over a century, but in 587 B.C. Jerusalem was overcome by Emperor Nebuchadnezzar of Babylon, taking many of the leaders into captivity in Babylon. After seventy years many from the House of Judah were released by Emperor Cyrus, and returned to rebuild Jerusalem. We read of their exploits in the books of Ezra and Nehemiah. This section of the Children of Israel, consisting almost entirely of the tribes of Judah and Benjamin, with some of the tribe of Levi, became known as the "*Jews*", and it was as a Jew that Jesus was born.

The Northern tribes, on the other hand, lost their identity. Some intermarried with the Assyrians and became known as the Samaritans, but the Northern Kingdom was never re-established.

Many Bible scholars have totally ignored this happening. They have regarded the Jews as the sole representatives of the Hebrew people. But this is to forget God's promises to restore both Houses. For example, the prophet Ezekiel wrote long after the destruction of the Northern House, but before the restoration of Judah:

"*For the word of the Lord came to me: Son of man, take a stick and write on it: 'For Judah and the Children of Israel associated with him'; and then take another stick and write upon it: 'For Joseph (the stick of Ephraim) and all the House of Israel associated with him'; and then join them together into one stick*". (Ezekiel 37:19).

This passage, like many others, points to the time when the whole of Israel will be restored. When the Jews returned after the captivity in Babylon it was only a partial recovery. They were still under foreign domination, and in A.D. 70 they were again driven out of their own land. It is only in our own century that we have seen the setting up of the Jewish State of Israel.

Maynard James studied all these Scriptures, and came to the firm conclusion that one day God would fulfil his word. But, if so, where were the lost tribes? If they are to be restored, then they must already exist. He studied the literature of the British Israel movement and became convinced that the British people, that is the English, Welsh, Scots and Irish, are part of the lost tribes.

I think he became attracted to these ideas in the Thirties, but it was not until the Forties that Maynard came into print on the subject. For example, in the January, 1945 he wrote: *"Some of us may believe that Britain is part of Israel"*.[10] For many years, however, he continued to write cautiously, as he did not want to cause unnecessary division. But by the Seventies he was less tentative; and he clearly identified himself with Reader Harris and Mrs George Sharpe who believed that the British people were part of Israel."[11]

Maynard was aware that many of his colleagues had little time for this theory, and he did not wish to alienate them unnecessarily.

He himself attended British Israel conferences at Swanwick and wrote from time to time in their periodicals; but within Holiness circles he kept a fairly low profile, while at the same time never being ashamed of his views. However, if the explicit view was low-key the implications were far reaching. It is probable, of course, that some of these emphases would have existed anyway, but they were certainly strengthened by his belief that the British people were part of Israel.

One such emphasis was that of race. Since the Second World War there has been a reaction against any form of racial thinking. This is almost certainly a reaction against the terrible extremes of Nazism, when millions of people were sent to the Gas Chambers on racial grounds. But the Bible has a lot to say about race. The verse *"In Christ there is neither Jew nor Greek"* is often taken out of context. While this is clearly our status in Christ, it does not mean that all races are the same, any more than it means that men and women are the same. God's plan was to and through the Hebrew people, and therefore they have added privileges and responsibilities.

Maynard believed that the British people were part of God's plan for the world. But he also realized that they had fallen far short of God's demands. He wrote:

"Fearful judgements are now falling upon Britain. They will continue until the nation, from the Queen downwards, sees not only its identity but, in consequence, realizes how great is its sin against the God of Israel. Until certain vile laws are expunged from our statute books and the nation repents in 'sackcloth and

---

[10] Flame, January-February 1945 p.9.

[11] Flame, March-April 1979 p.31.

ashes' before a Holy God, then no amount of planning and expediency will save us from the wrath to come."[12]

Maynard carried a great burden for his fellow countrymen, and he groaned for his nation. The sense of Britain having an Israel identity helped rather than hindered his prayers.

He believed that the Boer people of South Africa were also part of the same identity, and from time to time there were articles in the Flame which gave prayerful sympathy to the government of that country. I don't think Maynard ever supported full-blown apartheid, but he did believe in natural segregation. He wrote in 1970:

"A competent Christian leader spoke for many godly ministers when he told me that he felt it was the harsh application of the ideology of separate development that brought such pain and injustice to many peaceable and law abiding people."[13]

Maynard commended a benevolent government for bringing food and education to backward peoples, and he realized that primitive tribes could not suddenly be brought up to British standards by wishful thinking.

We have already seen how much Maynard admired Ian Smith in his fight for Independence in Rhodesia, and one Flame cover had a photo of the Rhodesian Prime Minister with Mrs Smith.[14] Views like this were no more popular in Holiness circles than amongst Christians generally. I myself heard one angry Church of the Nazarene minister berate Maynard for his *"reactionary views"*.

Another man he admired was Enoch Powell. Maynard agreed with him in his desire to curb immigration and also in his opposition to the European Common Market. They corresponded from time to time.

Such attitudes as these are regarded by many Christians as *"racial"*. I think if Maynard were alive he would reply: *"But we all belong to our race, and this carries responsibilities as well as privileges. Christ died for the whole world, and he loves all men. But in his love for them he chooses some to have special responsibilities. To deny this is to deny the whole Biblical drama."* In practice, Maynard was most gracious to people of other races, as his visits to Swaziland and India clearly

---

[12] March-April, 1979, p.25.

[13] Flame, May-June 1970 p.30.

[14] July-August 1976.

demonstrate, but he simply refused to believe God's purposes were identical for all nations.

Like most believers in the Israel Identity Maynard became very opposed to any idea of a secret Rapture of the Saints. Many Christians affirm that believers will escape the great tribulation, being "*caught up to meet the Lord in the air*". Maynard thought this went very much against Scripture; and although he was sometimes cautious in declaring his British Israel view in public he had no such hesitancy on the matter of the Rapture. For example, he wrote in 1959[15] that St. Paul foretold the "*being caught up*" as occurring at the Last Trump (1 Corinthians 15: 51, 52). The Rapture would clearly be linked with our Lord's Return in triumph to this earth as Paul had prophesied.[16]

Maynard fervently believed in our Lord's return. Like St. Paul, it coloured his whole life and thinking. He also believed that Christians would have to face many trials before that great event, and he felt the idea of being secretly whisked away was a real avoidance of the path of suffering to which God has called his people.

Even those who disagreed radically with Maynard's thinking on many of these issues admired his sincerity and graciousness. He was not afraid to swim against the tide, and he realized that many views were held simply because they were the fashion of the times. He was not afraid to be unfashionable.

It will be no surprise to our readers that Maynard very much favoured the British connection with Northern Ireland. He was grieved that the Protestants in that province had suffered terribly, and he thought that the British government should have taken a much tougher line with terrorism. He kept up a correspondence with the Rev. Ian Paisley, and although Maynard disagreed with many of his extreme statements he admired his courage and tenacity. When Louie was dying he received a lovely note of sympathy from Ian Paisley, which shows a very human side to that controversial figure.

Maynard's own attitude to the Roman Church may seem puzzling. For years the Flame thundered against the "*terrible system*" of Romanism, and Maynard continued with this line right to the end. Yet at the same time he came to know some

---

[15] Flame, November-December p.22.

[16] It is only fair to add that in the 1930's Maynard had accepted a Secret Rapture, e.g. Flame, June-July 1935, p.5.

Spirit-filled Roman Catholics, and had sweet fellowship with some of them. There was a nun in the Southport area who impressed him greatly, and he sent me some of her poems, which I published in my Parish Newsletter. But Maynard could not quite bring himself to print them in the Flame!

I think the reason was that he himself was puzzled. He really believed that the Roman Catholic Church had opposed or twisted many of the truths of Scripture, and he had seen a very ugly side of that Church in Colombia. And yet here were people who loved the same Lord as he did, and sometimes with the same burning zeal.

But Maynard was always a fighter for what he believed to be true; and if at times he felt he had to be cautious it was certainly not out of fear.

Throughout his ministry he faced controversy with courage and graciousness.

33. A student to the end!

CHAPTER NINETEEN
TILL DEATH US DO PART

The very early Eighties continued in much the same way as the late Seventies. Although Maynard himself was nearly 80 years of age, his life-style remained virtually unchanged from previous years. For example, his engagements in March, 1981 included visits to Emmanuel Church, Birkenhead; Gabalfa Baptist Church, Cardiff; People's Church, Liverpool; Parkhead Nazarene Church, Glasgow; and Cleveleys Baptist Church. During this year he was still writing vigorous articles in the Flame, and helping to organize the Southport Convention.

Many of Maynard's older colleagues had died, but Maynard still had some fine friendships. We have already mentioned a few of those who were close to him during his latter years, and several of these were outside the Church of the Nazarene, such as Denis Applebee, Stanley Banks, Ron Storey, and Gordon Taylor. Another friendship which deepened in Maynard's closing years was with Colin and Mary Peckham. Colin had entered into blessing on Maynard's visit to South Africa in 1954, while Mary (née Morison) had been one of the speakers at the very first Southport Revival Convention. Colin and Mary were now at the Faith Mission College in Edinburgh, and Maynard's visits to them became one of the joys of his old age.

But Maynard remained on very warm terms with many of the British Nazarene pastors, and he particularly admired some of the newer leaders. There was, for example, Herbert McGonigle who was a fine scholar and a future Principal of the Nazarene Bible College. He had been contributing to the Flame for many years, and was now taking his rightful place as one of the leaders of the British Church of the Nazarene. Peter Gentry was on the Editorial board of the Flame, and would soon be accepting a bigger role in the editorship. John Packard was another pastor who became a good friend of Maynard during his latter years; and we could mention several others. The pastors' wives also took Maynard to their hearts and always made a great fuss of him. But as well as developing new friendships, Maynard kept in close touch with his older colleagues, such as Albert Lown and Maurice Winterburn, and he often wrote them letters in his own hand.

The links with Albert and Maurice were very precious. They had come into blessing through his ministry, and they had both served with him in earlier days. Moreover, they were thoughtful

and compassionate men who time and time again reached out to
him in his old age.

But 1982 was to be a year of great change. Maynard would be
80 years of age in April; and on 16th January he wrote in his
diary: *"Louie not well"*. It was perhaps the first warning that his
partner was seriously ill. However, she continued to get about
and Maynard fulfilled all his preaching engagements.

On February 14th, 1982, Maynard's close colleague, Pastor
Glynn Thomas died very suddenly. He had joined the C.H.C.
shortly after the war, and his first pastorate was at
Walthamstow, Greater London. He had been brought up in
Swansea, the son of a bookie. He suffered atrocious health, being
both epileptic and deformed. But as a very young man he had
gone to a George Jeffreys Revival Rally and had been gloriously
healed and converted. The hunch-back disappeared as he walked
to the front to receive prayer! He had become a young evangelist
and trained at the Swansea Bible College. But then tragedy
struck. He was blinded through a road accident, and felt he
would never preach again. However, the Lord raised him up and
he continued his ministry as actively as ever.

Maynard came to know Glynn Thomas shortly after the War
and he was made a pastor of the Calvary Holiness Church. He
had strong Pentecostal leanings, and had a very real gift of
prophecy. However, he did not let the arguments about
"Tongues" disturb him - he just went on with his ministry, and
continued happily in the Church of the Nazarene. He and his
guide dog went all over the British Isles; and he himself travelled
overseas on several occasions to preach the Gospel. His blindness
rarely hindered his work. He gave an amazing testimony, which
never failed to move. In 1981 he attended a great Golden Jubilee
Service in Westminster Abbey of the Guide Dog Association. But
early in 1982, while still very active in his ministry, he was
suddenly taken to be with the Lord. Maynard preached at his
funeral on 23rd February at Leeds Dewsbury Road Nazarene
Church. There were seekers at this service as there had been at
Glynn's last service just a couple or so weeks previously.
Maynard called Glynn Thomas a *"Prince in Israel"* and his
passing was a sad blow. Glynn had shared Maynard's outlook on
the gifts of the Spirit, and his parting meant at least the
temporary loss of a very dear and understanding brother.

But a far greater blow was soon to fall. On 18th March Betty Scott[1] took Louie into Southport Infirmary for what seemed a routine visit. But Louie did not return home that day, as the surgeon told Maynard that she had a serious growth in the bladder.

Maynard was devastated. He wrote in his diary: *"Returned home desolate. 'Other refuge have I none, hangs my helpless soul on Thee.'"* Maynard usually had a good appetite, but now he had to force himself to eat.

I came to Southport on 25th March and again the following week. Dad and I had an interview with Mr Burgess, the same surgeon who had performed an operation on Maynard. He gave us a very gloomy report. They had been unable to remove the growth by surgery and radio-therapy was not recommended. It was virtually a death sentence. Mr Burgess also insisted that we should not tell Louie that she had cancer. This, of course, was the line taken by some of the older surgeons, and I still do not know if it was the right advice. It certainly meant a few months of pretence.

On April 2nd, Maynard and Louie's 52nd wedding anniversary, Louie was moved to Hesketh Park Nursing Home, in Southport. But on the evening of 11th April she had a very severe angina attack and was in extreme pain. Maynard was distraught and sent for me to come immediately. We saw the doctor at Hesketh Park the following morning, and he confirmed that Louie had suffered a nasty attack. I asked, rather naively, "Did she nearly die?" to which he replied: "It is a great pity that she didn't." It seemed a cruel remark at the time, but he obviously foresaw the terrible suffering that she was yet to undergo.

Three weeks later Louie arrived home in an ambulance, very frail but delighted to be home - how she hated hospitals! By the end of May she seemed a little better, and even got about a little. Kenneth came over from South Africa and this cheered her immensely. Maynard even felt free to fulfil an engagement in Northern Ireland.

At the end of June, Stephen flew from Kuwait to visit Louie. He was now working for Kuwait Airlines, as Laker Airways had collapsed. Louie was putting up a brave front, but things were gradually getting worse.

The exploratory operation on the bladder had made matters worse. She now needed to pass urine every few minutes, and it

---

[1] Daughter-in-law of George and Doris Scott. Doris had been one of Louie's closest friends.

became very distressing. Stephen was only able to stay for a short while, and soon after his return to Kuwait, things began to get considerably worse.

Louie now became confined to her bed, which was put in the front room.

Maynard was becoming very low in spirits. He had depended upon Louie so much, both as a partner in the ministry and also as a very efficient housekeeper. Louie had shielded him from domestic chores, and now it was becoming necessary for him to do some. He just couldn't cope. He wrote in his diary on 29th June, *"Oppressed in spirit. Dear Lord, help me."*

On 10th July the local doctor told Maynard that she thought Louie was dying. However, she rallied and Maynard was hoping and praying for a miracle. It was now necessary for Louie to have someone with her all the time, and some very good help was received from the Local Authority, from the Madam Curie Society, and from the Medicare Nursing Agency. Connie Winter and Betty Scott were also very attentive, and Mrs Winter sat with Louie for hours at a stretch, as well as seeing to much needed washing, as Louie's bladder was almost out of control. This caused Louie great distress of mind as well as body. She hated a mess or a fuss, but she was having to face both. However, Mrs Winter was unperturbed.

I tried to arrange for a housekeeper, and indeed managed to get the help of a good Christian lady. But Maynard's expectations were too high and she could not cope with his pressure. Friends urged us to put Louie in a Nursing Home, and indeed this is what Maynard now wanted. But Louie begged us to leave her at home.

By the latter part of July things were desperate. Not only was Louie very ill, but Maynard was nearly going out of his mind. He begged me to help put Louie in a nursing home; and on Wednesday 21st July I came over to Southport with this intention. But when I saw her I realized the end was very near, and I told my father that I would stay as long as I could. Each day she got worse, and it became very distressing. When she was only partly conscious she would try to get out of bed to use the bed-pan; and this would happen every few minutes. It was like watching a nightmare.

Even in this awful condition her kindly nature shone through. When I arrived she was so ill that she could barely speak. However, as I bent down to kiss her good night, she whispered: "Have you had anything to eat?"

On Saturday 24th July, Louie became unconscious and much of the stirring ceased. Even Maynard became a little more calm as he realized she was out of her pain.

On Monday morning I was preparing breakfast for my father and myself, when I had a great urge to go into mother's room. Now that she was unconscious it was not necessary to be with her every minute, but nevertheless I had an overwhelming desire to be there. I left my father to continue his breakfast and I went and sat with her. Dad (and I can hardly call him Maynard as I remember those precious moments) did not follow me, as he found it unbearable to see Louie in this condition. As I sat there I felt the sweet presence of the Lord. All the suffering was over, and a deep peace settled on her. Just at that moment Connie Winter walked into the room. I said: "The Lord is taking Mum now." Two minutes later Betty Scott walked into the room, and within seconds Louie had gone to be with the Lord. The sense of God's presence was awesome, and his timing was perfect. She had passed through the valley of the shadow of death, and the Lord had received her unto himself. It was 9.50 a.m. 26th July 1982. It was indeed a blessed relief. She had suffered so desperately for several months. No one who loved her wished it to go on. We were all, including Maynard, greatly relieved when she died.

Nevertheless Maynard was still having a momentous battle of faith. I was with him for part of this time, so I saw the battle myself. His diary reveals a little of his terrible perplexity. On the day of her death, he wrote in his diary: *"My darling Louie passed peacefully into the Lord's presence at 9.50 am. So grateful to the Lord for giving her such a peaceful period from Friday night onwards. My loss is very great!"* (his underlining). The following week, he wrote: *"I must confess to a day of terrible darkness and oppression. Dear Lord, what shall I do?"*[2]

Alongside the great relief that his loved one had passed out of pain was a very real perplexity, as well as of awful loneliness. How could God have allowed Louie to have suffered in this way? Why had she been so humiliated? I am not sure when exactly Maynard won through, but he later told me that he cried to the Lord in anguish, demanding to know why the heavenly Father did not prevent such suffering. And then, Maynard recalled, he seemed to hear the Father replying: *"I allowed my own Son to suffer and to be humiliated."* Maynard was much comforted, although the pain remained with him until his dying day. He

---

[2] Diary 4th August.

could not bear to have her photo in his room - the memories were so poignant.

The funeral took place in Christ Church, Southport, on the following Monday (2nd August), and the Church Service was conducted by the Rev. Stanley Banks, the son-in-law of the late J.D. Drysdale, the founder of Emmanuel Bible College. Stephen had flown from Kuwait, and was present with his family, as were Kenneth and Hazel who had travelled from South Africa. Cousin David broke off from his busy work as a London surgeon and also joined us in Southport. My own wife Glenys, daughter Ruth, and son Adrian were also with us. But it was much more than a family funeral for Louie was known all over Britain. Hundreds travelled to the Service.

The address was given by Gordon Taylor, who paid tribute to Louie for her stalwart support of Maynard's ministry and also her own gracious gift of hospitality and warmth, which he himself had experienced. Evangelist Dick Saunders was holding a Crusade in Southport at the time, and he and his team made contributions to the service, with a moving solo from Mildred Rainey. One unusual feature of the service was the singing of the well-known hymn *"Just as I am"* to the Welsh tune Llef.

The committal was at the public cemetery, on Duke Street, and the grave was very close to that of her dear friend Doris Scott. This part of the service was led by Dr. T.W. Schofield,[3] but with a great deal of impromptu worship, including the singing of *"In the sweet by and by"*. One great saint who made an effort to come many miles was Herbert Silverwood, the outstanding Methodist lay evangelist, who was still on fire for his Lord, although in his eighties. I shall never forget his singing around the grave. I learned afterwards that he was far from well, and indeed died a few months later.

Many paid tribute to Louie that day. She was loved for what she was - a saintly, hardworking, warm-hearted Mother in Israel. If she had a fault it was that she "spoilt" her family, including Maynard, but it was a fault of love.

Maynard now had to face life without his beloved partner. What would he do? Where would he live? These were indeed questions which needed facing.

---

[3] A leading minister of Church of the Nazarene in the British Isles.

CHAPTER TWENTY
LIFE WITHOUT LOUIE

As we have seen, Maynard was brought up in a mining community in South Wales. The men worked desperately hard in the coal pit and elsewhere, while the women folk looked after them and managed to keep the household going. The men very rarely did household chores - that was women's work! Louie had fallen into this style, especially as Maynard, although not a manual worker, worked very long hours and needed quiet and rest for his tremendous output. Louie not only cooked and shopped, but looked after the garden and managed the budget. When she died she left a domestically helpless partner. Even cooking a simple meal was a mammoth task. One solution might have been for Maynard to live with one of his sons and their families; and indeed this was earnestly considered. There were, however, great difficulties. Maynard was an extremely restless person and he did not seem able to fit into another person's home on anything like a permanent basis. I anguished about inviting him to live in Shrewsbury, an invitation which I think he might have accepted. But when he did stay with us, things were so difficult that I realized it would be impossible. It was not made easier by a very real clash of personality between Maynard and Glenys.

However, soon after the funeral the immediate problem seemed to be solved by Fred and Wendy Reynard inviting Maynard to stay with them at Altofts, near Wakefield. Fred was a lay leader of an independent Holiness Mission in the village, and Maynard had encouraged and supported them over the years. They were extremely kind to Maynard during this crisis, and he became the honoured guest in their home. There even seemed the possibility of this being a permanent arrangement.

Although Maynard was now eighty years of age, he still had many commitments in his diary. For example, at the end of August he took a series of services at the Oldham Tabernacle; this was followed by the Faith Mission Convention in Edinburgh, and the Southport Convention at the beginning of September.

It was in this style that Maynard lived throughout 1982, having a main base at Altofts but making several visits to his home in Southport, where he would stay for a few days, managing as best he could, and having a lot of meals out. He spent Christmas with Stephen and his family at Horsham, although this was a rather tense visit.

He had been invited to visit India; and after all the trauma of the past few months he felt this to be an impossible undertaking. But I encouraged him to go, as I felt it was just the enterprise he needed. After prayer he came to the same conclusion. It was to be a remarkable visit, and is best told in his own words.

"It was after long consideration that I accepted the invitation of the Rev. Joe Daniel, leader of the flourishing Laymen's Fellowship, to see for myself the revival movement so evident in parts of South India. So on January 20th (1983) I arrived in Madras, there to begin a five weeks' ministry which has deeply etched itself on my memory.

"Of course there were the well known sights, endless crowds, incessant traffic, deep poverty and tragic idolatry. To these must be added the humid heat and penetrating dust (due to a prolonged drought). But the Divine compensations far outweighed all the difficulties encountered.

"The first big event of my itinerary was the All-India Students' Retreat, which was held in the L.E.F. headquarters in Madras. From different parts of India they came - crowds of intelligent young men and women, eager to listen three times daily to the message of Full Salvation.......There came a sight I shall never forget, as groups of students scattered throughout the campus, to prostrate themselves before the Lord in ardent worship and fervent intercession....

"The night meetings were open to the public; and masses of simple, unsophisticated folk flocked in to hear the Gospel. An estimated three thousand persons were in the Sunday morning Service.....

"Following the Students' Retreat there came a seven hours' train journey to a place called Stuart Puram. It is a Criminal Settlement which, some years ago, experienced a mighty revival through the ministry of a spirit-anointed evangelist. Dangerous criminals - brutal, hardened men - were literally felled like oxen to the ground under the convicting power of the Holy Spirit. Glorious conversions to Christ, and miracles of healing, were witnessed, and the little town was transformed. As a result of that revival, a large Camp Convention is held annually in Stuart Puram.

"To preach on two successive mornings to an estimated five thousand people was an unforgettable experience. There were Hindus, Moslems, and idol worshippers among the masses who sat densely packed on the floor. To my surprise I was taken to a group of lepers who had their own quarters on the Camp grounds.

What a privilege was mine to minister to, and pray with, these seeking souls for whom Christ died!

"The next Camp Convention was in the heart of the city of Vijayawada, a crowded, noisy place where people sleep at all points in the congested area....... Then came the never-to-be forgotten visit to the city of Hyderbad, where the L.E.F. has a flourishing centre. Pastor Stephen Jubilee raj and his gracious wife are doing a mighty work for God in that important city.......
I am finishing this editorial in a place far removed from the almost unbearable heat.... After the strain of the past weeks it is paradise to be some 6,500 feet up in the Nilgiris mountains, at a place called Coonoor where large tea plantations flourish. Yet even at these heights the L.E.F. have preaching centres where crowds gather to hear the Gospel of Christ. Last night (Wednesday, February 16th) it was a change for me to give, instead of a sermon, a simple testimony to the transforming power of Jesus in my own life. How easy it was to testify to such a crowd of eager, longing souls!

"The sub-continent of India, with its 700 million people, presents a challenge and opportunity which must be taken........

"Just before leaving the Madras headquarters of the L.E.F. to fly back to England, I called in at the usual Wednesday Evening Prayer and Fasting Service. There I saw about four hundred men and women bowed before the Lord in earnest intercession and worship. There I realized anew the secret of the amazing fruitfulness of such a fellowship. They marched on their knees to revival blessing!" [1]

It was truly a wonderful visit of a doughty warrior to a needy and challenging land. What a thrill it was for him to witness again the mighty power of the Holy Spirit in perhaps even greater anointing than he had known it in the North of England in the 1930's! The visit was even more remarkable when we realize that he was still feeling desperately lonely and not very well.

He returned at the end of February to Southport, but it must have been a real anti-climax. He was far from settled, and within a month or so he returned to Wendy and Fred at Altofts. But it was becoming gradually clear that this could not be a permanent home. I think at first Wendy and Fred hoped Maynard would settle with them, but they soon realized that he could be very demanding and would not fit quietly into a corner. He had been

---

[1] Flame, May-June 1983, p.14-16.

centre stage for most of his life, and he found it almost impossible to be anywhere else.

With various preaching appointments, when he was usually given hospitality, and with short visits to Southport and to relatives and friends, the year wore on, but it was now becoming increasingly difficult. At the Southport Convention in early September he was taken ill and rushed into the local Infirmary, where they gave him X-rays, as cancer was suspected. It was the Golden Jubilee of the Salford Church on 18th September, and he shocked the doctors and nurses by insisting on travelling to fulfil his commitment. On the Sunday morning he preached with great power on *"Emblems of the Holy Spirit"*. He was very moved to be back with people he had known most of his life and where there had been such blessing in the 1930's. He preached again in the evening and there were five seekers. Those who saw him that weekend said he looked a shadow of himself, but preached with the same unction as of old. One observer was the Rev. Herbert McGonigle, who was honorary pastor at Salford at the time. He has written:

"The weekend was truly remarkable. He was very weak and frail and sat throughout the worship part of the three services. But when he stood up to preach, the Spirit came upon him and the transformation was astonishing. He strode the platform like a young man and the words just poured from him. On the Sunday evening we had eight members there who had been saved in the Salford tent in 1933, including Charlotte Middleton whose dramatic healing from MS turned the tide of that campaign...... It was an unforgettable weekend, with God's presence, tides of glory, powerful anointed preaching and seekers at the altar - a very fitting way to finish what was probably one of his last major preaching engagements." [2]

After this memorable weekend, Maynard spent several weeks at Altofts recovering his strength, and Wendy and Fred were exceedingly kind. In November he travelled to Bolton for their Jubilee celebrations, and again he spoke with great power although looking very thin and old. He was far from well, and after the Bolton meetings he was admitted again to the Southport Infirmary.

This time the staff were more convinced than ever that he had terminal cancer. There was no definite proof, but he had many

---

[2] Letter to the author, 8th April 1992.

of the symptoms. His diary records days of spiritual struggle, which he would mark with such entries as: *"A fight of faith today"*. Many who knew him found it strange that such an established Christian leader could have doubts and times of near despair. The triumphalists seem to think that if you trust the Lord everything is always fine. However, the reality is quite different, as Jesus himself knew. On the Cross he even thought the Father had deserted him. Maynard was himself going through such a period.

But he still loved to be with God's people; and I had to remind him that if he had really lost faith he would not love the things of God.

This seemed to help him and he continued to struggle on. The doctors told me they did not hold out much hope.

Then, to our utter amazement, he discharged himself and was admitted on a temporary basis to the Gables Residential Home in Southport, which was run by and for Christian people by the Aged Pilgrims' Trust. This move occurred during the Christmas period, and was a real fait-accompli. I was very disturbed and rang up the hospital. I was put straight through to his consultant, who did not seem too upset. *"Don't worry,"* he said, *"it is far better for him to die in surroundings he enjoys rather than in hospital"*. The Matron and staff at the Gables were extremely kind, indeed more than kind - they showed real Christian compassion.

Throughout January he was very poorly. and he remained nearly all the time in bed in the sick-bay. It did indeed seem that the consultant was right. However, at the end of January or early February he seemed a little better, and he announced that he had received a word from the Lord from Psalm 118 verse 18: *"I shall not die, but live, and declare the works of the Lord."* Soon afterwards he announced his intention of going to South Africa to visit Kenneth. It seemed an absurdity. He had hardly been out of bed, and was extremely weak. However, his doctor thought it would perk him up, and I agreed to take him. With the considerable help of the Rev. and Mrs John Packard from Bolton we managed to get him to Heathrow, and on Tuesday 13th March 1984 we flew to Johannesburg by South African Airways.

He was still far from well, but exhilarated by the prospect of seeing a country he loved, and spending time with Kenneth, and Hazel and his grandchildren, as well as seeing some of his old friends. Kenneth met us at the airport, where Maynard was put in a wheel-chair provided by the Air Company. The staff gave him every attention both at the airports and during the flight, and a difficult journey had been made easier.

Johannesburg was experiencing a heat-wave, and we sat for hours in Kenneth and Hazel's lovely garden, as well as visiting Kenneth's offices, which were in spacious grounds with swimming and tennis facilities. But after a few days Maynard began to get restless. Could we go to Cape Town? Peggy Dobbie[3] would put us up, he said. I was not so sure. Maynard was not now the travelling evangelist of a few years ago, but a sick and tired old man, who really should not have come abroad. But he persisted, and in the end we planned an itinerary. We would fly to a holiday flat near Durban for a few days, and then fly on to the Cape. Maynard rang Peggy who agreed to have us for a short time.

At the holiday flat near Durban we found ourselves almost prisoners. The weather had suddenly turned windy and cold, and Maynard was not well enough to move around. We were very pleased when it was time to travel to the Cape. We were met at Cape Town Airport by Pastor James Selfridge, who was a Minister of a Holiness group in the Cape. He was like an angel of light. He took us to the home of Miss Peggy Dobbie at Diep River, and offered to give us some of his precious time in showing us around the Cape.

We had a most enjoyable time, though Maynard was still unwell. Peggy was and is a great saint with a very hospitable nature. Her wonderful maid Hannah used to have times of prayer with her every morning, and the home radiated the presence of the Lord. There were also two paying guests in the home, who were engaged in Christian work.

On Sunday we worshipped at a local Anglican Church where Peggy played the organ. It was an exhilarating experience. The congregation,who were both white and coloured, were truly moving in the Spirit, and love simply flowed through the people. Maynard was very impressed, and we went again in the evening.

It was a thrilling experience for me. On the Monday morning I met the Anglican clergy for the whole area, and had a time of fellowship with them. On another day, Mr and Mrs Selfridge took me for a car ride around the glorious Cape, though unfortunately Maynard was not well enough to come. Cape Town itself is all that it is made out to be, with its towering mountain which can be reached by cable car. It was while in Cape Town

---

[3] Miss Peggy Dobbie, daughter of Captain and Mrs G.S. Dobbie.

that I met up with the Rev. Derek Pass and his wife Hazel. Derek was the son of Pastor Cyril Pass of C.H.C. days, and both father and son had come to work in South Africa. The father had worked with the Church of the Nazarene in South Africa (and had died a few months previously). Derek, on the other hand, had joined the Baptist ministry and was Principal of a Bible College, where he was doing valuable work among men of all races. Maynard was not well enough for most of these trips, but he did accompany us to the lovely neighbouring seaside resort of Fish Hoek. Here was a Brethren Guest House, and with cap in hand we asked if Maynard could stay there for a few weeks. In the end they agreed to squeeze Maynard in, and I think six weeks was the suggested length of stay, as I had to return to the U.K.

One highlight of the Cape visit must be recorded. While we were staying with Peggy Dobbie I was asked to speak at a nearby church with a largely coloured congregation. Maynard insisted on coming, although feeling very rough. When we arrived we were given a royal welcome. Many of the congregation had been blessed by Maynard's visit to their church in the Fifties, and the Pastor testified that it had been through Maynard's ministry that he, a coloured man, had been converted. It was a thrilling tribute to Maynard's ministry. After I had spoken, Maynard asked if he could say a few words. He staggered to the preaching stand, and then began to preach mightily. I could hardly believe my ears. Peggy told me afterwards that she too was equally overcome - he had been so weak all day!

I left the Cape, where I had been for about nine days, thinking all had been arranged for Maynard's next few weeks. But it was not to be! Maynard stayed a short time at the Guest House at Fish Hoek, and then decided he had had enough. I think he stayed with the Selfridges for a short time, before returning to Kenneth and Hazel in Johannesburg.

I returned to England at the end of March but Maynard flew home in June. He had kept a diary for years, but now it had many empty pages - a sign of his increasing weakness. From June to December there are no entries at all. He also began to find the Flame editorship too much of a struggle. He had kept it going during the dark days of Louie's illness and death and indeed throughout 1983, but in 1984 his ill health and weakness proved too much of a burden. There was a transition period when the Rev. Peter Gentry, who had been a friend of Maynard for many years, and was Pastor of Port Glasgow Church of the Nazarene, took over as Acting Editor, and he kept the paper going with much the same style and punch as when Maynard was in the chair. In September 1984 Peter took over the full editorship, and remains the editor to this day.[4] He has gradually put his own stamp on the magazine, but it is still recognizable as the vibrant paper that Maynard edited from 1935 to 1984.

Maynard's work as an editor and writer is very impressive and must compare with his preaching ministry. He never found writing as easy as preaching, for he loved a congregation and the immediate rapport which could come from the spoken word. However he was a pungent and skilful writer, and many found blessing through his writings.

1984, the year that George Orwell had depicted as the year of Big Brother, was certainly a landmark for Maynard. He now found he could not continue his full-time ministry. He was old, not well, and with no settled home. On his return from South Africa he stayed in several homes, including the Reynard's at Altofts, but never settling anywhere. I was very concerned about his health and asked the advice of David James my cousin, a surgeon in University College Hospital, London. *"It is quite clear that Uncle Maynard is suffering from gall-stones"*, said David. *"How can you tell?"* I asked, *"you have not even seen him, and the doctors are convinced it is cancer"*. *"No"*, replied David, *"from what you have told me it is gall-stones"*. And gall-stones it was! These had been giving him trouble for some time and had passed unnoticed in the Southport Infirmary. I wrote to Maynard's Doctor in Southport, but as Maynard was always on the move she could not do much. Shortly afterwards, however, while he was staying with Mrs Kathleen Toft at Leeds,[5] he was rushed into Leeds Infirmary. This time gall-stones were diagnosed, and after treatment his health improved considerably, although he was never to recover his full strength.

But the other main problem remained - that of his virtual homelessness. I felt then and indeed still feel, some guilt about this. I can only say that it seemed at the time impossible to do more than was done. I gradually came to realize, however, that some desperate measures must be taken, and this came to a head

---

[4] The Rev. Peter Gentry has now retired from Pastorate duties, and is living in Weston-Super-Mare.

[5] Mrs Toft is the widow of the late Pastor Harry Toft, who had been a vibrant C.H.C. Pastor.

while Maynard was staying in Majorca for a few months in the spring of 1985.

While Maynard was abroad I prayed hard and searched diligently for the right place. It seemed to come. I was offered a place for Maynard at the Wirral Christian Centre in Birkenhead. He would have a large room and all meals provided. Moreover it was a place of rich Christian fellowship. Some Elim pastors and laymen had realized the vision of a Centre where the needs of both old and young could be met. With great faith they bought the old hospital on Woodfield Road and converted it into an Old People's home, a Chapel for the Elim Congregation, a Lunch-club, a Youth centre, etc., etc. It was, and is, a remarkable place. When I saw it it was very new - or at least very new in its refurbished state - and was shortly to be officially opened by Princess Alexandra. It seemed just the place for Maynard, and was only a very short distance from both the Emmanuel Holiness Church and the Emmanuel Bible College where Maynard had so many links.

Then came the blow. Maynard had a stroke at the Guest House in Majorca. He had been very upset by what he had seen in the home in Palma and decided to confront the Pastor in charge. From what Maynard told me later it was quite a meeting. I do not know the rights and wrongs of it, but Maynard was convinced that Satan had got a hold of the place. The confrontation upset him a great deal, and a day or two later he had a stroke. He arrived back in Cardiff with slight paralysis and impaired speech.

Stephen and Kenneth were both in the U.K. at the time, and as Maynard seemed to be recovering from the stroke very quickly we pressed him to take the offered place at Birkenhead. He appeared to agree and we actually arrived one day in May with the hope that he would stay. But at the last minute he resisted the idea, and asked Kenneth to drive him to Altofts. We thought we were back at the beginning!

34. The old warrior at Dewsbury Church Golden Jubilee, 1984.

CHAPTER TWENTY-ONE
THE LAST ENEMY

Maynard remained at Altofts for about a fortnight, and at first it looked like an impossible situation. However, Stephen had a long talk with him and finally persuaded him to give the Wirral Christian Centre a try. Maynard's attitude was rather a resigned one. He didn't particularly want to go, but if the Lord was leading in that direction then he would not disobey.

And so Maynard returned to the Wirral. After a few difficult weeks, he settled down very well and actually told me he was happy. He joined in several of the activities of the Centre and also made new friends from Emmanuel Church.

The Hutchinson family, with husband Trevor and wife Ruth, and their two sons, often invited him to their home, and he took a prayerful interest in their welfare. Others also in the town were very kind to him; and for a time all seemed well. But, after about a year or so, he became unsettled again and took himself off to Oldham where he begged lodging with Mrs Ruth Jackson, one of the stalwarts of the Oldham Assembly. It became obvious that things had not been right for him at the Centre during the previous weeks. A new warden was running a different regime which did not suit Maynard. To this, however, must be added Maynard's natural restlessness. Even when Louie was alive he used to get agitated if he was not active with preaching engagements.

Stephen and I had a long talk with Pastor Paul Epton who was the Director of the Centre. He and Mrs Epton had been very kind to Maynard; and they very much wanted Maynard to return, and promised closer supervision, with the hope of a place in the new nursing home being built at Leasowe, near Moreton, as soon as it was ready.

Maynard was enjoying his time at Oldham, and took some convincing that Mrs Jackson could not keep him on a permanent basis. Looking back, however, we can be grateful that he had this short respite in a Christian home in a town that he dearly loved and where the Lord had so mightily blessed in the past. His diary had become very spasmodic, and his very last entry before he stopped writing in it altogether was in Mrs Jackson's home, and is dated 11th May 1987:

"Rain in morning. Wrote to Leonard Ravenhill. Reading and prayer with Mrs Jackson. Very feeble physically - but rejoicing in the Lord. 2 Cor. 4:16."

It was written in his own lovely handwriting, and showed little sign that he was now very old and had fairly recently suffered a stroke.

After a period of a few months at Oldham he returned to Birkenhead, and the Eptons were as good as their word, and he was indeed better looked after. Moreover, within a few months, the new nursing home at Leasowe was opened and Maynard was transferred there. He was given a lovely room and was cared for by properly trained nursing staff, who took his foibles in their stride.

He quite liked the new surroundings, but he began to long for a return to Southport, where he and Louie had lived so happily. He had been on the waiting list at The Gables for sometime, and had been offered a place a year or so earlier; but at that time he seemed well settled, and decided not to accept the offer. However, we kept him on the waiting list, just in case. While Maynard was at Leasowe I approached the Aged Pilgrims' Trust, and he was again offered a place.

He was due to move at the end of May 1988, and all preparations were made. He appeared a lot better, and on Sunday evening, 15th May, was taken by friends to the Emmanuel Church at Birkenhead. The preacher was Gordon Taylor, who had been such a close friend to Louie and Maynard and had given the address at Louie's funeral. His sermon at Emmanuel Church that Sunday evening was on the theme of *"Victory over Death"*, and the closing hymn was *"When the roll is called up yonder I'll be there"*.

The next day, however, Maynard became ill, and by Friday morning it became clear that he was very ill and probably dying. I was sent for, but for four hours they were unable to get me, simply because the phone was not ringing properly. Eventually I got the message about 6 o'clock in the evening, and by 8 o'clock I was at his bedside. He recognized me - just - but was fading fast. The nurses were deeply moved, as he had been praising the Lord as he was getting weaker. He had made it clear that he was going to his heavenly home, and all his fears and depressions disappeared. He had always been afraid that he would let the Lord down by his death. He had had some grim moments during the past few years, and at times his faith seemed to be very fragile. But when the real test came he was ready. One nurse told me she had never experienced anything like it and it had brought her much nearer to God.

I slept the night of Friday 20th May in his room, and there were no more signs of consciousness. At about 9 o'clock the next morning he slipped peacefully away, and the earthly battles of a great warrior were over.

I managed to get in touch with Stephen, who that morning was at Macclesfield, about fifty miles away. Within a couple of hours he was with me, and was very moved by the peace in our father's face.

Maynard had lost consciousness on the anniversary of Louie's birthday, 20th May, 1988, and died the following morning.

The immediate question now arose: Where should the funeral take place? Obviously the burial would be in Southport, at the Duke Street Cemetery where Louie was buried, but several venues were suggested for the main service. In the end, in consultation with Stephen, we decided to ask Pastor Epton if the Service could take place in the Wirral Centre Chapel, just below where Maynard had lived for a couple of years, before he was moved to Leasowe. We also asked Pastor Epton to lead the service; as well as inviting several pastors from the Holiness movement to take part. Which pastor should we ask to give the address? It was suggested that we should have several tributes, but I resisted this. There should be one address only. After prayer and thought the name of Dr. Albert Lown came into my mind. He had been with Maynard on the early treks when Albert was a very young man. Moreover, he was a good speaker and, most important of all, a true man of God. When I rang him he readily agreed, counting it as one of the great honours of his life. Very quickly all the arrangements were made for the service to take place the following Friday, 27th May.

Kenneth and Hazel flew over from South Africa, and nearly all close relatives prepared to meet at Birkenhead. I was receiving telephone calls and messages from all over the country, and also had to prepare the service. I had some years previously discussed hymns with Maynard, and the ones chosen were: "In heavenly love abiding" to the tune "Penlan", the old holiness hymn, "Called unto holiness", and "Love Divine" to the tune "Blaenwern". As arranged the service was conducted by Pastor Paul Epton. Maynard's old friend Maurice Winterburn read the lesson, which was made up of selected passages of Scripture, including verses from 1 Corinthians 15. Others taking part were the Rev. Herbert McGonigle, Principal of the Nazarene College at Didsbury, Dr. T.W. Schofield, now Regional Director of the Church of the Nazarene, and the Rev. Stanley Banks, the son-in-law of J.D.

Drysdale, and himself an evangelist and teacher. Dr Lown gave a masterly and moving address in which he compared Maynard to St. Stephen and John Wesley, and as an epilogue to the sermon the Rev. Denis Applebee read John Bunyan's tribute to *"Mr Valiant-for-Truth"*.[6]

It was a wonderful service. One Elim pastor from the Christian Centre wrote to me afterwards to say that Albert Lown's address was the finest he had ever heard. Another very happy feature of the service was the blend of Holiness and Elim folk. Maynard had struggled for many years to bring better understanding between these two fervent groups, and his funeral itself was a testimony to that stand, as the congregation was made up of holiness folk from all over the country, as well as a number of the people from the Christian Centre who had come to know and love Maynard.

The Committal was at the grave in Southport, and as it was twenty miles away, a much smaller group attended this ceremony, which was led by Maurice Winterburn, who had been a loyal friend to Maynard over many years. He was a former I.H.M. Minister, but in his later years had been ordained into the Church of England. He never lost contact with the holiness movement, and was a regular speaker at conventions. He was now retired from parochial ministry, but was as active as ever. He had visited Maynard at Birkenhead, and was often dropping him an encouraging line. It was therefore very appropriate that Maurice should take the Graveside Service. Prayers were led by the Rev. John Packard, another good friend of Maynard. Informal singing broke out during the course of the little ceremony as a great warrior was finally laid to rest.

Although it was sad in some ways that Maynard had now left this life, it was also a time of joy. His work on earth had clearly finished, and he had been finding each day a struggle for some time. He had died in triumph, and he had been laid to rest surrounded by many loved ones - and he was loved by many people.

Immediately after the Committal those who had journeyed to Southport joined together for a happy time of fellowship and refreshments at the home of Mr and Mrs Ron Storey who had been good friends of Maynard and Louie. It was a family reunion as well as a meeting of friends, and the youngest member of the family was present - little Danny, aged 18 months, Maynard's

---

[6] See Appendix for a summary of Dr. Lown's sermon.

great-grandson.[7] Among the friends of Maynard was one with very special memories. He was Mr Kenneth Price, whose home Maynard had shared in the formative Cardiff days before Maynard went to Cliff College.[8]

For several weeks the tributes and letters continued to flow in, and there was a further opportunity for both mourning and celebration with a Memorial Service at Morley Church of the Nazarene, on 8th July, at which the preacher was the Rev. Colin Peckham, the Principal of the Faith Mission College, Edinburgh.

How can we sum up the life of Maynard in a few words? We have already referred to Albert Lown's sermon (see Appendix), but there were also several other testimonials which were published in the Flame. We shall quote briefly from just a few.

"Maynard James' passing has meant that one of the great leaders of the holiness movement has gone to his reward. There was a real sense of Christ's resurrection victory at the funeral service..... He was the first Editor of the Flame and carried on this job for nearly fifty years. Although primarily a servant of the cause of holiness.... he had a wide influence in other areas" (Maurice Winterburn).

"The warmth of his home life, with his beloved Louie providing a well-provided table, was like a little bit of Wales transported into exile across the border......... to kneel in prayer with the two of them was to travel the world and forget time........ As the small coffin was laid to rest with that of his beloved, he had returned to Southport. His three sons stood with many of his spiritual sons to bid him farewell. The sun shone brightly as spontaneous singing broke out. I somehow felt I could hear an echo from the hills from far away Bargoed..... hills that had echoed to the cry of a young boy from Bargoed who yielded to the mighty claims of God and caused us to thank God for Maynard James, preacher, pioneer, and prophet" (Denis Applebee).

"One of the outstanding features about him it seems to me, was his recognition and appreciation of the many facets of Christian truth and experience, a quality which has always been reflected in the Flame magazine....... He was a "catholic" in the true sense of that much-abused term." (Pastor Noel Brooks, Conference Superintendent of the Pentecostal Holiness Church).

---

[7] The child of Sara and Tom, daughter and son-in-law of Stephen.

[8] Kenneth Price works for "The David Press" which exists to express Christian love for the House of Israel and to spread universally Messiah's truth.

"To be with Brother James when he prayed was a deeply moving and unforgettable experience, whether in public prayer in services and conventions or special times of prayer in missions and fraternals or in family prayers in the home....... he was great man and a true Prince in Israel" (Herbert McGonigle).[9]

There was also a very warm tribute from the General Superintendents of the Church of the Nazarene in America, with whom he had clashed over charismatic gifts a few years earlier. But to quote further tributes would be tedious. I would, however, like to make my own final comments both as Maynard's son and also as a student of his life and works.

He was one of the most single-minded men that I have ever met. I have heard of other single-minded people who have done outstanding things - such persons as Winston Churchill, Field Marshall Montgomery, and (on a rather different level) Enid Blyton. Churchill could be desperately rude to those who worked with him. Montgomery was at times very selfish, and one of his adjutants has described him as a great soldier and a poor man. He could be ruthless in order to achieve his ends. Enid Blyton could blot out her family for days while she was engaged in her writing. I think many great people have this single-mindedness, and very often it is very difficult to live with. My father could show some of these traits, and his family often suffered. However, he nearly always had about him a sense of the presence of God, and Christian love usually counteracted his faults.

Along with Jack Ford, Leonard Ravenhill, and Clifford Filer he blazed a trail for Holiness in Britain which is without parallel this century. He was, as Noel Brooks has described him, a true catholic, with kindred spirits in many denominations. He even found them in Roman Catholic circles, much to his own embarrassment, as he always hated the system of Romanism.

His editorship of the Flame for nearly fifty years was a mammoth achievement and touched thousands of lives. But in this, as in many other aspects of his work, he owed a great debt to others.

We have already paid tribute to Louie's work, and the wonderful support she gave to Maynard. There were many others I would like to thank, but the list would be too long, and I should forget to mention some very important people.

In any case, it is "to God be the glory". He took a young lad from a Welsh valley and made him into a prophet for holiness.

---

[9] All the above quotations are taken from the Flame, September-October 1988.

He was aptly named "Holiness James" at College, and under God he did perhaps as much as anyone in the Twentieth century to further Scriptural Holiness.

His grave-stone sums up my feelings for him both as father and also as a Christian leader; and in this I am joined by my brothers Stephen and Kenneth. It follows the inscription to our mother Louie:

> *Also her husband*
> *Maynard G. James*
> *Died 21st May 1988, aged 86 years*
> *A man of God, a leader of men*
> *And a pioneer for Holiness*
> *"He loved to hear his Lord spoken of,*
> *And wherever he saw the prints of his*
> *shoe in the earth, there he coveted to*
> *set his foot too."* (Pilgrim's Progress)

The fire of the Holy Spirit truly burned in Maynard James; and he always wanted to be "red-hot" for his Lord. His prayer-life was one of his great secrets. He was determined to keep the flame of prayer alight, and he was a man who spent many hours on his knees. He was truly "A Man on Fire".

****

35. *The author at his parents' grave.*

36. *The Rev. Dr. Albert Lown, in younger days.*

APPENDIX

THE FUNERAL SERMON
(Adapted from Dr Albert Lown's Address)

Maynard, the single Christian name by which the Rev. Maynard Gordon James was known, is eloquent of the unique intimacy of heart and spirit he unfailingly gave to his colleagues and converts, and to the numerous people who loved him from many denominations.

He was a beloved husband, father, grandfather, and great-grandfather, as well as evangelist, teacher, church-planter, prophet, writer, and father-in-God. He was a friend to me and my family throughout the whole of my ministry; and the same could be said of many others. Large though this congregation is, it is but a microcosm of the worldwide fellowship who would covet to be here, and who were touched by Maynard.

When he died last Saturday, the Rev. Herbert McGonigle declared: *"Truly a great man and Prince in Israel has fallen this day"*; a cry which is echoed in the hearts of us all.

I would liken his departure to the triumphant translation of Elijah and the victorious, Christ-like death of Stephen. Like Stephen, Maynard James was filled with Holy Spirit from the commencement of his ministry to its close at 86 years of age.

He lived for the anointing unction of the Holy Spirit that bathed his soul and sermons. He breathed prayer, so much so that often *"his face shone"* as he stood between the living and the dead. Revival was his spiritual life-blood; he had a burning passion for God and Souls.

The same authority that was evident in Stephen's ministry - *"they could not resist the wisdom with which he spoke"* - was the hall-mark of Maynard's pulpit and open-air ministry, whether the theme was the saints of the Old Testament, the Song of Solomon, the Second Blessing, or the Second Coming. He sought always to exalt Jesus as Saviour, Sanctifier, Lord and Coming King.

He was the master of the altar call, and he pleaded as an ambassador - in Christ's stead. As a young sanctified chemist, or as a college student and president, pastor and international evangelist, a barren altar call was rare in his ministry. Multitudes responded to the call, found the joy of salvation and entered into the Canaan experience, as they were counselled and prayed through. The Rev. Maurice Winterburn and myself entered into the blessing of a clean heart and the sanctifying grace of the Holy Spirit through his ministry - and we shall be eternally grateful.

As Stephen *"looked steadfastly to heaven and saw the glory of God and Jesus standing on the right hand of God"*, so Maynard James maintained an incredible optimism in all circumstances, and often in impossible situations. He was a man of the Upward Look, for he truly loved the Man at God's right hand; and while Jesus was praying for him nothing could daunt his spirit. I never had fellowship with him without being truly blessed, and feeling a better person.

Again like Stephen and our blessed Lord, prayer was the master habit of his life, his joy and his refuge. His prayers are remembered in many homes, and by all ages. To the end, in spite of physical weakness - mercifully terminated on the 250th anniversary of Charles Wesley's conversion - he walked through death's shaded valley and entered heaven with praise and prayer:

"When Christ shall come with shouts of acclamation.
And take me home, what joy shall fill my soul!"

This was his constant acclamation, until on Saturday, 21st May at 8.00 a.m. he passed into his rest, and could then proclaim: *"My God, how great thou art!"*

He was indeed a 20th Century John Wesley, with incessant labours, a daily constitutional walk, a regular habit of afternoon rest, and ability to relax and rest in the will of God. Like Wesley he could feel and grieve, but refused to fret. Both were founders of churches and open-air preachers; and in Maynard's pilgrimage there was too a "Holy Club", with Leonard Ravenhill, Jack Ford, Clifford Filer, and himself. They honoured him as we honour them - each and together lived for holiness evangelism. The parallel with Wesley extends to the very last night on earth, when Wesley repeated: *"God with us... God with us... God with us"* and *"I'll praise... I'll praise... I'll praise"*. Maynard too died praising his Lord, as those who tended him can testify.

If Maynard had recorded a last message to be read at his funeral, it would surely have been the final concern of Elijah: *"Ask what I will do for thee before I am taken from you"*. To the united request: *"Give me a double portion of thy spirit"*, Maynard would have replied: *"You have asked aright, but look beyond my translation to glory, and your loss to the God of my life and ministry. His Spirit is fully available to face the Jordans I have crossed, to meet the sons of the prophets - a new generation - and to serve the church and nation I have served."* If Maynard's prophetic warnings and writings over the greater part of this century had been heeded, Britain would be much nearer to God than she is today.

May the mantle of Maynard's spirit, the anointing of God's Spirit, be ours - ministers and laity alike, family and friends. May the Holy Spirit be a loving comforter to a loving, mourning family circle, especially in the months that follow these first tribute-filled days. When the lovely floral tributes have faded; and the flowers of memory have not fully bloomed, and when the sense of loss is deepest, may you then, Paul, Stephen, Kenneth, and yours, see the Lord high and lifted up, yet comfortingly near. May you hear his voice and find sorrow turned into compensating, nobler service, may you, may we all:

> "Trace the rainbow through the rain,
> And feel the promise is not vain,
> That morn shall tearless be."

> "We shall meet him in the morning.
> Just within the eastern gate."

And now the Rev. Denis Applebee, a close friend and colleague of Maynard, will read a passage from Pilgrim's Progress which more perfectly expresses the sense of love and loss that unites our hearts.

"After this it was noised abroad that Mr Valiant-for-truth was taken with a summons by the same post as the other, and had this for a token that the summons was true, That his pitcher was broken at the fountain. When he understood it, he called for friends, and told them of it. Then said he, I am going to my fathers, and tho' with great difficulty I am got hither, yet now I do not repent me of all the trouble I have been at to arrive where I am. My sword I give to him that shall succeed me in my pilgrimage, and my courage and skill to him that can get it. My marks and scars I carry with me, to be a witness for me that I have fought his battles who now will be my rewarder. When the day that he must go hence was come, many accompanied him to the river-side, into which as he went he said, Death, where is thy sting? And as he went down deeper he said, Grave, where is thy victory? So he passed over, and all the trumpets sounded for him on the other side."

MAIN SOURCES

<u>Books and Documents</u>:

"In the Steps of John Wesley" *Jack Ford (Church of Nazarene)*

"The Flame" *from 1935 to 1988*

M.G.J.'s Unpublished Papers and Diaries

M.G.J.'s Books:

    "Evangelize" *(Pilgrim Publishing House)*

    "Facing the Issue" *(Pilgrim Publishing House)*

    "When Thou Prayest" *(Beacon Press)*

    "I Believe in the Holy Ghost" *(Bethany Fellowship)*

"What the Holiness People Believe" *Jack Ford (Emmanuel Bible College)*

"J.D. Drysdale" *Norman Grubb (Lutterworth)*

"Ye shall be Witnesses" *the Oldham Tabernacle 1932 - 1972*

"The Story of Trekking" *Albert Lown*

<u>Other Sources</u>:

Personal knowledge and recollection

Conversations and correspondence with relatives and friends of M.G.J. including:

    Mrs Beryl Cole *(cousin)*

    Mrs Emily James *(sister-in-law)*

    Mr Stephen James *(son)*

    Mrs Margaret Shepherd *(relative)*

    Mrs Elenor Ainscough
        (friend and former missionary, now deceased)

    The Rev. Dr. Albert Lown
        (friend & colleague, now deceased)

INDEX

(Place names are printed in italic)

LIST OF PHOTOGRAPHS